BEYOND BAPTISM

A GUIDE FOR NEW CONVERTS

BOOKS AUTHORED OR COAUTHORED
BY ELAINE CANNON

Adversity

As a Woman Thinketh

Baptized and Confirmed: Your Lifeline to Heaven

Be a Bell Ringer

Bedtime Stories for Grownups

Boy of the Land, Man of the Lord

Called to Serve Him

Corner on Youth

Eight Is Great

The Girl's Book

God Bless the Sick and Afflicted

Heart to Heart

Life—One to a Customer

Love You

Merry, Merry Christmases

The Mighty Change

Mothering

Mothers and "Other Mothers"

Not Just Ordinary Young Men and Young Women

Notable Quotables

Putting Life in Your Life Story

Quote Unquote

The Seasoning

The Summer of My Content

The Time of Your Life

Turning Twelve or More: Living by the Articles of Faith

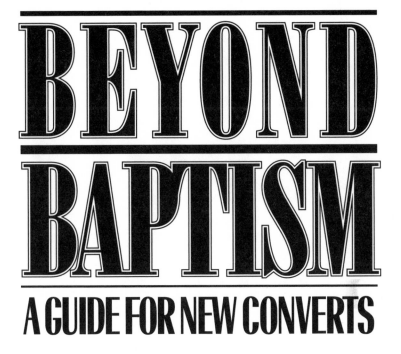

BEYOND BAPTISM

A GUIDE FOR NEW CONVERTS

ELAINE CANNON

Bookcraft

Salt Lake City, Utah

Library of Congress Catalog Card Number: 94-71250
ISBN 0-88494-911-7

First Printing, 1994

Printed in the United States of America

Contents

Acknowledgments... vii

Prologue.. 1

1 We Latter-day Saints.. 5

Section One: The Blessings of Membership

2 There Is a Plan! 11

3 Our Venerable Heritage... 16

4 The Restoration of the Gospel in Our Day............................. 19

5 The Blessings of Membership 23

6 Making the Ideal Real... 37

7 The Inspired Church Structure... 44

Section Two: Living by the Gospel's First Principles

8 Come unto Me 59

9 Faith in the Lord Jesus Christ.. 64

10 Christ's Call to Repent 69

11 Christ's Redeeming Love 75

12 True Baptism.. 82

13 Confirmation and the Gift of the Holy Ghost 89

Section Three: What You Need to Know

14   The Light of Life...   97

15   The Articles of Faith... 103

16   The Standard Works 116

17   Questions and Answers... 120

        Epilogue... 130

        Glossary 132

Acknowledgments

I acknowledge and commend you, a seeker after truth, to whom this book is dedicated.

Every author should be so blessed as to have a bright, helping spirit like our son Tony. For him and for the support and perspective of special friends and loved ones—some born in the covenant and some adult converts to the Church—I am deeply grateful. I am thankful as well for the inimitable Light of the Lord.

Bookcraft is committed to the spiritual education and motivation of us all. I value this opportunity to work with them. And plaudits to its staff of tasteful experts in editing, designing, publishing, and marketing *Beyond Baptism*.

May all of this work together for your good.

Prologue

Life offers an infinite range of choices, a menu of dazzling options for emotional rewards and lofty projections of dreams. It is a wonderful world to live in and an exhilarating time to be alive!

What father hasn't held his newborn child in his arms while gazing at the night sky and tantalizing the baby with stars to reach for?

What youth has remained unmoved when studying the planetary system?

Who hasn't listened to the reports of space explorers and marveled how these *trained scientists* stumble in their efforts to express their feelings about earth and space? The fragile gemlike quality of this sturdy earth, when viewed from outer space, leaves one almost overwhelmed. And there is an acute sense of universal unity as borderlines disappear with distant vision.

To say the least, we are part of an awesome universe, an obvious miracle of creation. There is order here, eternal sameness, and yet predictable variety. Somewhere out there—beyond, behind, above—somewhere is God! The Creator!

Yet in all this grand perspective, the greatest of God's creations is the human being—invisible to the space explorer but known by name and virtue to God. The creator of multiple worlds and incredible natural adornments thereon, God values his children above all, fashioning a suitable universe especially for them.

The children sing about all this with such eloquence and enthusiasm it stirs one's faith!

> Whenever I hear the song of a bird
> Or look at the blue, blue sky,
> Whenever I feel the rain on my face
> Or the wind as it rushes by,

Whenever I touch a velvet rose
Or walk by our lilac tree,
I'm glad that I live in this beautiful world
Heav'nly Father created for me.

He gave me my eyes that I might see
The color of butterfly wings.
He gave me my ears that I might hear
The magical sound of things.
He gave me my life, my mind, my heart:
I thank him rev'rently
For all his creations, of which I'm a part.
Yes, I know Heav'nly Father loves me.

(Clara W. McMaster, "My Heavenly Father Loves Me,"
Children's Songbook [Salt Lake City: The Church of Jesus
Christ of Latter-day Saints, 1989], pp. 228–29; used by
permission.)

God gives us commandments to teach us how to be truly happy.
However, we have our agency, God-given so that we may select how
we will deal with each situation we encounter. Choice is essential to
growth and fulfillment. Right and wrong, good and evil, smart and
stupid, essential and merely delightful—all these and more mark the
battlefield.

Baptism and confirmation in the Church of Jesus Christ are the
beginning.

It is in this church that the fulness of the gospel provides explanations to the mysteries of creations, the wonders of relationships, the
rewards of God's gifts in life! It is easy to worship God when such an
awakening burns in our souls.

Though our worship is very personal, after we are baptized and
confirmed we take up a life of growing in an understanding of the
miracles of God, of space, of choice, of being committed to God's will.

Beyond Baptism is a handbook for those who have been converted
to the Lord Jesus Christ, who have found a place in The Church of
Jesus Christ of Latter-day Saints, and who feel committed to an inspiring lifestyle. After we are baptized and confirmed we have a new
chance at a pure, God-oriented life. We become part of a ward family,
too, which provides ready-made friends who can quickly become

loved ones. The significant steps of baptism and confirmation open a door to a life of activities that are accompanied by blessings almost past imagining! Life itself is different. New values replace former ideas. Even familiar traditions are enhanced, like honoring Sundays, strengthening family life, exercising wise professional options, and coping with heartbreak moments. Yet other doors open and shut as the purpose of a covenant life unfolds.

Within the covers of *Beyond Baptism* there are comforting answers to plaguing questions. There is a glossary of LDS church language and terms. There are explanations of Church administration and programs. There are reminders of the glorious promises and blessings God has in store for his children. And there are scripture references that explain and support every part of the Church experience for its members.

Beyond Baptism is a lively probe for adults into what lies beyond baptism and confirmation. Children of eight and over who are being baptized will want to read a companion book called *Baptized and Confirmed: Your Lifeline to Heaven.* In fact, many adults have been awakened by this basic explanation and the illustrative stories. However, *Beyond Baptism* is focused on deeper doctrine and a wider range of topics. Its material is directed to the new Church member who is seeking success in this new life as a Latter-day Saint, but it is also valuable for an established Church member to review.

Life is a great drama, an exciting adventure. It is a spilling of moments that sum into eternity. Ready or not, the Millennium will come! Naturally, thinking people who are moved upon by the Spirit want to know more and more about the truth of it all.

By way of personal witness, I must forthrightly state that the institution of The Church of Jesus Christ of Latter-day Saints has been affirmed in my mind by both study and experience. It is a God-given and guided organization like no other on earth. This is proven in its fruits. It is at once humbling and exhilarating to know that God is the Heavenly Father of us all, to know that he lives and that his Son Jesus Christ lives and is our *necessary* Redeemer, our wise and wonderful Friend who is always there for us. I am increasingly grateful for the gift of the Holy Ghost that can follow only baptism and confirmation in God's church. I cherish my life, my work, and my special experiences in the Church. I pray that this may also be the witness of readers of *Beyond Baptism.*

1

We Latter-day Saints

A Latter-day Saint could be anyone in the world. There are close to six billion people in the world struggling to get their view of the stars. And each one is different from any other.

Someone once said that if all of us on earth stood side by side and held hands, the line would stretch almost 153 times around the equator. (If we all held hands there might be more peace on earth, as well.)

As distinctive as each of us is spiritually and physically, all six billion of us have much in common—not the least of which is absolute brotherhood with a long heritage that *precedes* Adam. It has been said that Latter-day Saints are unique. If this is true indeed, can we be picked out in a crowd of six billion?

Actually a Latter-day Saint can be blind, deaf, disabled, or physically gifted; black, brown, brick, yellow, or pale of skin; old, young, vibrant, passive, studious, colorful, or conservative—just like others on the street.

Profession, work, or duty won't set a Latter-day Saint apart either. You see, a Latter-day Saint is a shoemaker in Milan, a woman with a vessel on her head in Africa, a bookbinder in Queens, an organist in Austria, a cattle rancher in Australia, an opera star at the New York Metropolitan, an English bobby or a lady-in-waiting, a world-famous heart surgeon, a leader in NASA, a custodian in Macao, a man and his wife walking narrowly past Dachau, a border guard between Russia and Finland, a movie star, a politician, a scientist, a librarian, an author, a model, a Samoan mother, an artist on the Rive Gauche, an archaeologist in Ephesus, a Mexican cab driver in Merida, a basket weaver in Fiji, a tile worker in Portugal, a mula maker in Colombia, an athlete from southern Utah, an astronaut in space, an emigrant worker in San Diego, an orderly at Massachusetts General Hospital, a tailor in Miami, a tour director in Hawaii, a professor at Stanford, a tutor in Japan, a former nun, a former priest, a former drunk, a musician, a designer, an anchorwoman, a diplomat, a millionaire.

In some ways we Latter-day Saints could be anyone on any street anywhere.

Yet to compare our church with any other religion or philosophy is to emphasize basic differences in belief about the nature of God, where mankind comes from, the purpose of life on earth, and where we are going when we are finished here.

Latter-day Saints are Christians. When we are baptized into The Church of Jesus Christ of Latter-day Saints, we take upon us the name of Jesus Christ. We covenant to serve him with all of our might, mind, and strength. In a weekly sacrament service we happily renew those covenants to obey his will. The rewards of such faith and lifestyle bring peace, joy, and security.

This book considers covenants of worship and action as well as the actual way we as Church members live now—what we do and what we do not do. It is about our mind-set and our assurance of hope in Christ, come what may. It is about the way we marry, the way we rear our families, the way we feel about them. It is about our personal discipline and the way we respond to our leaders. It is about our heritage and our keen interest in beauty, truth, and the saving principles of the Lord's gospel. Paramount in each of our lives is how we make choices, face adversity and death, spend the Sabbath, serve others, and mark our personal progress. For Latter-day Saints, this is somewhat different from the rest of the world because continuous revelation from God has so enlightened our way. We each learn different things from different challenges, and we may be on different spiritual levels for a time, but before our lives are over, we all have the opportunity to learn something marvelous of God's ways; we can all recognize the perfection of his principles leading to life eternal!

Today the world wraps around *all* people its tentacles of trends, terrorism, media, music, ethnic food and clothing, literary translations, political transplants, philosophies, and ideologies. Latter-day Saints resist such tentacles. Our yardstick for measuring values is linked to our knowledge of the sacred nature of God, the fulness of which includes covenant children to help share his saving gospel with others.

Latter-day Saints are the fulfillment of prophecy. We are they who have been "gathered unto the Lord" and his church from every kindred, tongue, and nation across the world from Africa to Alaska, Thailand to Puerto Rico, Seattle to Salem, and beyond.

Since the beginning of time, God has had covenant people help in his work to bring to pass the immortality and eternal life of mankind. We do not ignore our tie to former covenant peoples. They had a work to do as well as their personal lives to play out. Our tie to them is long, strong, and real. Our debt to them is deep. And our covenant obligation to continue the work they spent their lives in is no less than their own.

We Latter-day Saints are known not alone by how we look or speak or what our work is but also by what we deeply believe. This is echoed in God's call to us as recorded in Doctrine and Covenants 115:5; "Verily I say unto you all: Arise and shine forth, that thy light may be a standard for the nations."

The person who accepts this call then becomes part of an impressive and caring community of disciples of Jesus Christ. And life will never be boring, ordinary, or purposeless again!

SECTION ONE

The Blessings of Membership

2

There Is a Plan!

Where did we come from? What was our beginning? Was there a life before this one? What happened then? Does it make any difference now? What's it all about anyway? These are among the questions directed most frequently to The Church of Jesus Christ of Latter-day Saints, to whom God has revealed the plan of salvation, or the plan of happiness, for his children.

Letters asking about human destiny flood Church headquarters. People are intensely concerned and seek satisfying answers to what life is all about. They are not the first. Great thinkers through the ages have pondered this matter. Voltaire was concerned as to how men passed from barbarism to civilization. Other philosophers have wondered how people make passage from spirits to mortals and mortals to spirits as in death. Some quote the teachings of Paul as they answer the questions with a question: "Know ye not that ye are the temple of God, and that the Spirit of God dwelleth in you?" (1 Corinthians 3:16.)

The classic poets have had their say, too. Milton and Longfellow, among many others, have spent their energies and talents on trying to explain the mysteries of life. Wordsworth showed an uncanny prophetic vision when he wrote these familiar lines:

> Our birth is but a sleep and a forgetting:
> The Soul that rises with us, our life's Star,
>   Hath had elsewhere its setting,
>   And cometh from afar:
>   Not in entire forgetfulness,
>   And not in utter nakedness,
> But trailing clouds of glory do we come
>   From God, who is our home
>
> (William Wordsworth, "Ode: Intimations of Immortality
> from Recollections of Early Childhood").

We Latter-day Saints understand that mortals come "not in entire forgetfulness, . . . not in utter nakedness." We also understand that we come into this life with preparations from the heavenly home on high. We are equipped to perform a mission on earth and are provided an agenda that includes temptation, trials, joys, learning, growing, and honing our spirits and proving ourselves worthy for eternal life when this earthly estate is done. We recognize with thousands of others that, thanks to the sacrifice of the Redeemer, at some point after death every person will be resurrected. Exaltation—living in the presence of God—is a status we can be granted after proving our knowledge of and obedience to his will and his word.

In that premortal home in God's very presence, we were prepared for the grand adventure on earth. We learned our first lessons there. We were enriched by him in all knowledge. Such a belief in a divine premortal education encourages a mighty self-worth and confidence to go purposefully forward! Among those who do not understand this truth, confusion understandably reigns.

Over the generations since Jesus lived on earth—especially through the Dark Ages and the great apostasy from truth—this perspective of where we came from and why we are here on earth was lost. Such apostasy from God and his will can come through sin as well as ignorance. Through the restoration of the gospel and the establishment of The Church of Jesus Christ of Latter-day Saints, we have whatever answers are to be had about the life before this and the life after this. Though full details have not been revealed, the fact is that we lived in the presence of God. With us were the spirits that either will inhabit or have inhabited the mortal bodies of all men and women who have ever lived or will yet live on earth. *We are all spiritual offspring of God our Heavenly Father.* Thus we are all brothers and sisters with a spark of the divine in us. This realization affects the way we feel about others. This is true whether or not we are blood relatives, Latter-day Saints, citizens of the same country, strangers, neighbors, or fellow worshippers. As the Apostle Paul wrote, "The Spirit itself beareth witness with our spirit, that we are the children of God" (Romans 8:16).

But even in that premortal home there wasn't perfect peace, because we could exercise our agency. In a developing drama were God our Heavenly Father; Jesus Christ, who was God's firstborn in the spirit; and Lucifer, or Satan, brilliant, arrogant, a "son of the morning" of our Heavenly Father.

A Council in Heaven

A council was called with all the spirits of Heavenly Father's family, including you and me. Heavenly Father presented to us his plan for our eternal progress and joy. Lucifer objected and proposed an alternative approach that would curtail our agency and give him glory above the Father. It was rejected. Lucifer rebelled and was cast out by Heavenly Father. Jesus, on the other hand, offered to carry out God's plan according to his will and to give the Father all the glory. Jesus, as his part in the plan, became Heavenly Father's Only Begotten in the flesh and our Redeemer.

But never underestimate Satan's cunning and intelligent mischief as he has forever after sought to thwart the Lord's plan. Forever after there has been war between the followers of Lucifer and the disciples of Christ. Make no mistake, this is real. We are "free to choose liberty and eternal life, through the great Mediator of all men, or to choose captivity and death, according to the captivity and power of the devil; for he seeketh that all men might be miserable like unto himself" (2 Nephi 2:27).

A third part of the hosts of heaven followed after Lucifer and joined in his efforts to pull mankind into his destructive web. They share his fate of having been denied a physical body and a life on earth and are his corps of warriors in the great battle. Satan's forces attack the most sacred opportunities in the Lord's plan—procreation, marriage, and family relationships—with tactics that include infidelity, premarital sex, irresponsible parenting, greed, and jealousy—whatever renders man incapable of eternal life with Father. Choice is touted as the right of man, but Satan makes no mention of accountability for decisions or of the need for repentance. Ultimately his followers are lost in abject misery. The streets of the world today are full of such pitiful persons.

We must consider that God's plan allows for bad things to happen to good people and good things to happen to people who have made bad choices. The difference is that when you are on the Lord's side and follow his principles, you will be ushered, shielded, and strengthened in time of need and given comforting understanding through the Holy Spirit. Others do not have this consolation!

Life is about growing, and growing happens more surely during troubled times when you keep close to the Lord. You then accept with patience, humility, and a long-range view of purpose the sorrows that come. You then can say not "Lord, why me?" but rather "Thy will be done."

Perhaps you have been like many others who haven't realized that premortal life was a preparation for this earthly experience and that our response there influenced our life here, just as this mortal life is a preparation for life beyond the grave. This understanding is unique to the restored Church of Jesus Christ. Others simply do not have this doctrine, this fulness of truth that gives purpose to our existence. The plan of salvation is the fulness of the gospel of Jesus Christ.

Latter-day Saints strive to learn the irrevocable laws of eternity and participate in the disciplines, endowments, and ordinances revealed for our benefit. When followed, the plan of redemption ensures for us the joy of closeness to the Lord through both the good times and the struggles. With the Lord as the center core of life, as our understanding of him increases, our love and trust and peace increase as well. We can always turn to him for needed nurturing.

The Plan

The Church of Jesus Christ is based on the plan of salvation. From the Church's inspired structure to member involvement in all its programs. The plan is implicit.

Latter-day Saints do have something additional, something correct and complete, to share with the world, even those who already believe in Christ. Church members believe that the worth of souls is understandably great before God because they understand the origin and destiny of those souls. Each person should therefore have the chance to learn the details of God's plan and belong to the safety of such caring membership as that found among the Latter-day-Saints.

Not surprisingly, a distinguishing feature of faithful Latter-day Saints is a sense of personal mission to share with others the benefits of the Restoration—true knowledge of God, an understanding of life's purpose, the promise of eternal relationships and a happy sense of belonging, and direction against sticky temptations and devastating problems that often need not occur.

There are at least two things to keep in mind as you try to learn more about the gospel and participate in the plan: First, you have the privilege of being tutored by the Holy Ghost—that precious gift bestowed upon you during confirmation after baptism (see chapter 13). You have the responsibility to strengthen your individual testimony and closeness to the Lord and to govern your life more completely (and therefore more easily).

Second, be mindful of the keen interest the devil will take in you now! Once you embrace the Lord's gospel and put a foot to the path marked by the plan—once you step into the light—you may be tested and tempted and troubled in a forceful way. Beware, lest it be fatal! But if you trust in the Lord and heed the promptings of the Spirit, you will not be tried beyond what you can endure successfully with the Lord's help. In a time of trial, all your antennae should be up to heed the warning and tune in to God's signals.

In everything can be good growth, personal progress, and increased witness that God lives and that his plan for us is a holy and joyful opportunity.

Try it and see for yourself!

3

Our Venerable Heritage

Each of us is influenced by a complex result of forces.

Each of us has an environmental heritage, the result of where and with whom we live, study, work, and worship.

Each of us has a biological heritage that through the magic mix of genes provides each of us with our unique appearance and physiological makeup. Our body houses the eternal and unique spirit within each of us that governs how we will use our God-given agency to make choices, to act or react.

We also have a spiritual heritage. Those of us who have been baptized and confirmed have a special heritage passed on through priesthood power and religious training that gives us power to rise and shine as God's covenant children.

The Church is the one institution that can help you understand all of this. Such information can change your life as well as your perspective! You perceive that your father, mother, children, and even difficult personalities or enemies are your brothers and sisters. We are all spirit children in our Heavenly Father's family, dating back to premortality. Not one of us "owns" another, even our own biological children. And when some older Saints talk about "going home," they seem to have an uncanny hindsight that prepares them for future heavenly relationships.

Our venerable religious heritage begins with Adam and comes down through the ancient prophets and heads of dispensations to our latter-day prophets in The Church of Jesus Christ of Latter-day Saints, beginning with Joseph Smith.

It is safe to say that we owe some of our religious opportunities to those who colonized America and established the Constitution of the United States. Latter-day Saints know this was all under the hand of God, because only in a free land could there be an adequate base for the worldwide spread of the gospel of Jesus Christ and the unfolding of the plan of salvation for all mankind.

Our spiritual heritage moves through the Bible, the Book of Mormon, certain other sacred writings, and the records of civilization as we have access to them. We read there of the continuum in covenants, commandments, and promises in the gospel and see evidence of similar traditions regarding reverence for life, sanctity of marriage, birth, family, duty, death.

God's plan of life has been in operation since the beginning of time, although it has not always been received by wayward or wicked people. Jesus, the Son of God the Father, the God of the Old Testament and Redeemer of the New Testament, has been watching over the affairs of mankind. Life on earth has developed somewhat according to mankind's choices, according to their closeness to God and their readiness to obey his will and word. He has taught all that is necessary for exaltation. Soon after he lived on earth and was crucified, the generations of the Church weakened. There was a falling away. But in this last dispensation of the fulness of times, the foundation has been laid for the final scenes of man's history on earth.

A religious dispensation is a divinely appointed ordering of affairs of mankind. It is the period of time when a certain prophet gives out or explains God's will to His children on earth. Every prophet of God has tried to help people understand the plan of salvation.

True prophets of God always have been teachers of truth among God's children on earth. Each prophet in his day has had a particular and important mission to fill, and each mission has had a different focus from that of others. As Latter-day Saints, we feel a sacred debt to the ancients whose lives and times, teachings and personal strengths add light to our own seasons and Church assignments! Included among these ancients are Adam, Noah, Abraham, Moses, and Lehi.

And what of Jesus? What part of our long spiritual heritage do we

receive from him? Though in following chapters I will discuss the
Savior's unique role, I want to note here the benefit we enjoy of
Christ's example—his compassionate ministry to the downtrodden,
the unclean, the haughty, the saint and sinner alike; his doctrine of becoming a peacemaker and his promise to the peacemakers and the
pure in heart; his urging for us to pray always and to love our enemies. There are his moments of inimitable power when he controlled
the elements or confounded the rabbis in the synagogue as a youth.
We are indebted for a heritage of understanding about Gethsemane,
Golgotha, and the garden tomb—the Atonement, the Crucifixion, and
the Resurrection—surrounded by the heartrending reality that Christ
was the Son of God and had power to stop his own suffering. Instead,
he laid down *his* life for *us*!

Although the Bible contains information about the early prophets
and their contributions, latter-day scriptures and continuing revelation give beneficial clarification. This includes a correct view of the
Great Apostasy, which ultimately necessitated a restoration. This
restoration, of course, was under the guidance of God through Joseph
Smith, who stands at the head of this last dispensation, and through
those men chosen by God to succeed him as prophets in their day and
for their specific missions in the unfolding fulness of the gospel plan.

In spite of the prophets, people over the generations have used
their free agency to listen to Satan, to follow their own selfish pursuits,
and to deny God. When whole cultures follow this path, wickedness
and destruction inevitably follow, as history has proven.

How great a blessing it is, then, to live when the fulness of gospel
truth has been restored! You are associated with a church that has ancient ties and eternal promises. You are related to *all* people—whether
they realize this or not! This church has been established in this day
under the direction of the Lord Jesus Christ to bless us all through the
restoration of truth. Joy and eternal life await all who will accept it.

People who believe in God, try to obey his commands, and call
upon him are blessed. You will discover this is true in startling numbers among the Latter-day Saints you might meet across the world,
whatever their cultural background. Signs follow true believers, according to God's promises. I witness this is true as part of our venerable spiritual heritage.

4

The Restoration of the Gospel in Our Day

The early Apostles taught that the future would bring a long-awaited "restitution of all things." Peter said that God had spoken of this "by the mouth of all his holy prophets since the world began." (Acts 3:21.)

The Church of Jesus Christ of Latter-day Saints contains the fulness of the gospel of Jesus Christ. Although there is often some truth, some continuum of Christ's teachings from two thousand years ago among other religious organizations, only the Latter-day Saints enjoy the untarnished truth, plus continued revelation from God.

The exhibits at Church information and visitors' centers usually include a display to help seekers after truth understand the sequence of and serious deprivations caused by an apostasy in belief, or a falling away from understanding God's plan and purposes.

By the time young Joseph Smith was praying to God in the early 1800s for help in what we now call the Sacred Grove, mankind was ready for a restoration of truth. So much had been lost along the way that gave meaning, order, depth, and joy to life!

Churches, for whatever reasons history can supply us with, no longer held the answers for the meaning of life and its challenges for the lay member. Most individuals felt little support from the system.

By Martin Luther's day, Christian churches had significantly veered from the teachings and manner of Christ.

Christianity in that period can be likened to a mirror—a mirror that through the carelessness of mankind is smashed into many pieces. The broken pieces of the mirror are scrambled for, snatched at. And even if there were efforts made to try and assemble and patch the pieces or "reform" the mirror, it would not give a true reflection because of the distortion.

God withdrew his power from the earth because of those who had perhaps unwittingly smashed the mirror.

The Christian world needed more than a reformation. Please don't misunderstand. The reformers are to be praised for their insight, their restlessness about what man, in the name of God, perpetuated in the church tradition. But the gospel mirror was broken, and the only way to reach truth would be through a new mirror: God would need to completely reissue his truth and restore his principles, priesthood, ordinances, and purposes.

With the answer to Joseph's prayer the process got under way.

In 1820 Joseph, a sensitive and thoughtful fourteen-year-old, realized that he had a problem. He loved his large family, but there was disunity among them. They were going to different churches to worship. Joseph was old enough to make his own decision, but he was confused about it. He studied the Bible for guidance and found direction while reading James 1:5:

> If any of you lack wisdom, let him ask of God, that giveth to all men liberally, and upbraideth not; and it shall be given him.

Joseph arrived at the conclusion that he must ask of God, if he was to settle the question he had in his mind.

For his special prayer, the young man went into a grove of trees near the family farm about two miles outside of Palmyra, New York. He knelt and prayed. At first he was overcome by the forces of evil to the extent he felt he would be destroyed. But he continued to cry out to God, and suddenly he was delivered from the unseen enemy that held him bound. He writes:

> At this moment of great alarm, I saw a pillar of light exactly over my head, above the brightness of the sun, which descended gradually until it fell upon me.

It no sooner appeared than I found myself delivered from the enemy which held me bound. When the light rested upon me I saw two Personages, whose brightness and glory defy all description, standing above me in the air. One of them spake unto me, calling me by name and said, pointing to the other—*This is My Beloved Son. Hear Him!*

My object in going to inquire of the Lord was to know which of all the sects was right, that I might know which to join. No sooner, therefore, did I get possession of myself, so as to be able to speak, than I asked the Personages who stood above me in the light, which of all the sects was right (for at this time it had never entered into my heart that all were wrong)—and which I should join.

I was answered that I must join none of them, for they were all wrong; and the Personage who addressed me said that all their creeds were an abomination in his sight; that those professors were all corrupt; that: "they draw near to me with their lips, but their hearts are far from me, they teach for doctrines the commandments of men, having a form of godliness, but they deny the power thereof." (Joseph Smith—History 1:16–19; see also verses 13–15.)

The world was never the same again.

Heaven had begun to open its mysteries to mankind again.

God the Father and Jesus Christ had made themselves known as distinct beings!

The Holy Spirit flooded the earth like a benevolent river.

People were enlightened. The human mind was quickened.

Knowledge flowed forth and progress leapt ahead.

Inventions for the benefit of mankind were developed.

Understanding replaced much confusion.

Impetus to right social wrongs increased.

The time had come for God to again take an active role in establishing his kingdom among his mortal children. Mankind would have again all that was necessary for joy in this life and the life to come. It was the dawning of a brighter day when the last and greatest of all God's dispensations for his children burst over the world.

Of course, the true test of a historical event is not just how it looks at the moment of happening, but what its fruits are, what effect it has on the future.

The First Vision and Deity's subsequent tutoring of Joseph Smith was a high moment in history, and the fruits of the Church through the years validate its firm position as the institution to protect and promulgate the true gospel of Jesus Christ on the earth at this time.

Line upon line the Lord's blessings unfolded. Christ came again. Angels appeared with messages from God. Resurrected beings assisted in restoring the holy priesthood and the authority to use it in God's name for the benefit of his children. And there was the miraculous acquisition and translation of ancient records that contain such beautiful clarifications of the gospel while testifying to God's constancy and purpose with his children.

The Church has also had its buffeting, persecutions, and required martyrdom. Satan continues to orchestrate evil against the people and programs of the kingdom of God on earth! However, like the children of Israel, we too have had our exodus—a trek across the wilderness to a barren salt desert. We have built our cities, our places of worship, and our temples for sacred work as revealed by God. We have established our storage facilities to care for the needy in time of crisis. Church statistics indicate a high percentage of member devotion and participation. This is of course a natural consequence of the quality of the lives led by Latter-day Saints and of their individual spirituality. The beauty and the goodness of children coming from sturdy families prove the worth of the Church's teachings.

The world is forever in the debt of Joseph Smith, prophet of God over 150 years ago.

5

The Blessings of Membership

Beyond baptism and after confirmation comes life in The Church of Jesus Christ of Latter-day Saints.

Life begins again. How will it be for you?

Of course, beginning life as a Latter-day Saint doesn't mean you will abandon all the good things about your prebaptism life. It simply means that the unpleasant mistakes and misunderstanding are wiped out. You can forget them and move forward to become what you were meant to be and to do what you were meant to do.

Jesus explained his own mission during New Testament times in this way: "I am come that they might have life, and that they might have it more abundantly" (John 10:10).

If you were a Christian before you converted to The Church of Jesus Christ of Latter-day Saints, you accept that statement about abundance. But knowing what you know now, with your new enlightenment through the gift of the Holy Ghost given you at confirmation, you know that Jesus' ministry in Jerusalem was only the beginning. He has also come to earth in our dispensation! He has revealed truths, hopes, and promises for our day as well.

Life under these circumstances, blessed by these truths, is truly more abundant.

What does all this mean for you?

It means that you can have the assurance that you are being instructed, guided, and enhanced through life according to the plan that the Creator *of you* has *for you*. This plan provides not just a quantity of advantages but also a higher quality, custom designed for your life as a child of God on earth. The details are available only through the Church; thus, the Church is the means to this abundant life.

The church you've joined will be different in many ways from the experiences you have had before. The restored gospel of Jesus Christ is housed in a system or institution that has come about through continuous revelation to meet your needs today (see chapter 2).

First Blessing: The Holy Sabbath Day

Sunday as a member of the LDS church will be different from the way the world usually spends it. It is a time of spiritual emphasis. It is a day of rest, a day of drawing close in worship to God, from whom all blessings flow! The Sabbath is the day the Lord has made for man to pay his devotions to God and to allow His Spirit to shine over the weekly demands on the physical being. As a Latter-day Saint, you try to prepare your meals and groom yourself in a way that shows that you respect the Lord and this gift of life he has given. You avoid entertainment and the world of work that could be done during the rest of the week.

By keeping the Lord's day holy, as a Latter-day Saint you will be blessed temporally and spiritually. That promise is detailed in Doctrine and Covenants 59:9–19. As this revelation indicates, the Sabbath was established so that Church members could keep themselves unspotted from the world by going to church, a house of prayer, and partaking of the sacrament. Through the sacrament you renew your covenants with Christ to always remember him; to keep his commandments that he has given you so you may always have his Spirit with you. No matter what else befalls you in life, yours can be abundant and full of joy.

Second Blessing: The Structure for Personal Growth

The gospel can be seen as a theology of behavior and experience. The Church's programs, principles, and ordinances are manifest in a carefully structured system for personal growth and spiritual strength.

The sacrament is blessed and passed to all worthy members weekly at a Sunday worship service. In addition the following group meetings are held on Sunday:

- *Sunday School,* with combined male and female members, the youth usually being divided into classes by age groups
- *Primary* for children under twelve
- *Relief Society* for women over eighteen
- *Young Women* for young women between twelve and eighteen years of age, usually divided into three age groups
- *Aaronic Priesthood* meetings for young men between twelve and eighteen years of age, divided into three age groups corresponding to quorums of deacons, teachers, and priests
- *Melchizedek Priesthood* meeting for men, divided into quorums of elders and high priests

There are also a variety of weekday experiences for social, cultural, physical fitness, and leadership training that provide opportunities to apply gospel principles to life. A person's whole being benefits from Church membership.

Third Blessing: Valuable Relationships

The worship services, classroom study, and interaction through the organizational structure of the Church stimulate a variety of relationships. The Spirit is clearly evident not only because of the type of meetings, the gospel lessons, the fulfillment of the promise that the Lord would be with his children but also because of the spirit about the people who attend. They have accepted the gift of the constant companionship of the Holy Ghost, as you have. It shows. You can feel it as happy, radiant, committed people gather to learn, worship, and help each other.

Life can become very rich when you have such a variety and number of people with whom to interact. The Church's emphasis is on families—including God's family—where churchgoers are called "brother" and "sister" and children are welcome indeed. Special events are also planned to meet the needs of singles. No one is left outside the Church family.

The support system that such a structure and philosophy generates is remarkable. You'll make new friends, caring friends, friends with the same high ideals, eternal goals, and lifestyle as you. Ward families are organized according to neighborhood boundaries. Though you may be from different walks in life with different pursuits or you may move to a new community as a stranger, you will know exactly where the members of the congregation are headed. You live by the same standards and seek the same ordinances. Whether old or very young, you learn to call each other by name. You not only *feel* included, you *are*! People, as well as families, who sing together, play together, and pray together are more likely to stay together. You are brothers and sisters blessed and bound by the inimitable love of Christ.

During the Sunday meetings, the prayers, choir, speakers, and teachers, as well as the special musical numbers, are drawn from among the congregation itself. This provides both opportunity for personal growth and information about other people in the ward.

Once a month, usually the first Sunday, a special worship service called a fast and testimony meeting is held instead of the regular sacrament meeting. This is a favorite meeting with the Saints because so many soul-satisfying things happen. In this meeting, a name and a blessing is given to each new baby, and members stand up as the Spirit moves them to testify of their knowledge of God and to acknowledge their gratitude for blessings. Families sit together for this and all sacrament meetings. Compassion and love fill the hearts of members. People greet each other warmly after the meeting because of the mellowing influence of the Spirit there.

Fourth Blessing: Increased Intelligence

Increased intelligence is a goal of Latter-day Saints. In Doctrine and Covenants 130:18, 19, we read:

> Whatever principle of intelligence we attain unto in this life, it will rise with us in the resurrection.
> And if a person gains more knowledge and intelligence in this life through his diligence and obedience than another, he will have so much the advantage in the world to come.

As you attend your Sunday meetings, you will grow in your understanding of the whole gospel of Christ.

Remarkable manuals or study guides are prepared by the Church and translated into many languages. They are geared to the needs of each age group. The Gospel Doctrine class, for example, studies each year a portion of the standard works in a four-year repeating cycle: (1) the Old Testament, (2) the New Testament, (3) the Book of Mormon, and (4) the Doctrine and Covenants and the Pearl of Great Price.

Even the children to the age of twelve learn doctrine and are trained up in the way they should go (see Proverbs 22:6). In a revelation given through the Prophet Joseph Smith, the Lord stated, "I have commanded you to bring up your children in light and truth" (Doctrine and Covenants 93:40). The Primary organization of the Church is dedicated to aiding parents in the accomplishment of this mission.

The Primary lessons are directed to preparing children for growth in the Church. For example, those children preparing to be baptized at age eight learn the important matters surrounding this ordinance. Those who are approaching age twelve and are preparing to move out of Primary will focus on living by the Articles of Faith and will memorize them as a constant reminder of important aspects of their belief and behavior.

The Primary has its own opening agenda when the children are given opportunities to give brief talks, pray publicly, or participate in others that give them confidence. Later they separate into their age-group classes for gospel instruction.

Fifth Blessing: In Constant Touch

A variety of Church experiences helps us keep in touch with God and with each other. This is an ever-increasing blessing. Structured Church meetings or service projects help us develop an increased closeness with God. Here you have a variety of opportunities to meet people, to interact, to learn from them, to share your own good ideas and feelings, to grow in affection and respect as you serve each other.

The Church helps each person develop in all ways through programs that include activities for the following: cultural insight, physical fitness, athletic competition, group camps and field trips, genealogical research and name extraction, welfare services, musical events, social dances, ward dinners, youth firesides, homemaking skills, temple preparation classes, and temple excursions to do the vicarious work necessary for those who have died without the blessings of the saving ordinances.

One of the greatest blessings in this area comes because of the Church structure that calls for representatives of the bishop to visit in the homes of the members of the ward.

Visiting teachers are pairs of women who serve as companions representing the Relief Society and who each month call upon assigned ward sisters. They deliver a message from the Relief Society to give the women spiritual comfort, understanding, and sometimes a gentle nudge in the right direction! They see to special needs. These relationships usually develop warmly and become meaningful to both the visitors and the sister member. This is particularly important when the sister is homebound or is struggling with loneliness or temporal need. Visiting teachers help during times of death as well as birth, illness, or heartbreak. They prepare meals and brighten lives. They give more than compassionate service. They are angels for a time, guided by inspiration as an answer to prayers.

Similarly, two members of the priesthood are assigned to each home to represent the bishopric as home teachers. They watch after in a loving way the two or three families to which they are assigned. Often these brethren will provide spiritual reminders, appropriate temporal assistance, and practical guidance if desired. They become very important to a family and can be called on to help give blessings to heal sick family members, to officiate in a baptism of another family member, or to help in the naming and blessing of a baby or the confirmation of a child who has been baptized. The home teachers usually call ahead to make an appointment to visit the family, who, now alerted, can be ready to put aside their activities and gather to be instructed and to pray with the home teachers. A warm relationship can develop that is often long and important to these people.

Sixth Blessing: Prophetic Guidance

Oh, the gladness of being part of a God-inspired organization!

Prophetic guidance and continuous revelation from God come to Church members through the prophet and President of the Church. There is power, there is accuracy of direction, there is light and understanding in being led by an anointed mouthpiece of God. Only he holds all the keys from God for the salvation of the Saints during his day. Therefore, the President of the Church is revered. His word is heeded by the faithful.

The prophet is the only one to receive direct revelation from God pertaining to the entire Church. Each worthy member, however, can receive personal revelation from God for his or her own life. The pattern for receiving such revelation goes something like this: you should first learn to face a problem or an option in light of the scriptures—the word of God in print. Then in sincere prayer, seek guidance from God to learn his will for you. Be humble and repentant. Then keep your eyes, ears, and heart open for inspiration.

Seventh Blessing: Leadership Training

There is no doubt about it, Latter-day Saints from earliest childhood are given unusual opportunities to learn how to conduct meetings and prepare an agenda. They keep historical records and manage budgets. The variety in public, organizational, and volunteer service fosters this growth.

Faithful Saints pray constantly for the Lord's help in such undertakings. They also turn repeatedly to the Lord's revealed standards as goals for any Church service. Through such experiences, leadership training builds confidence, increases people skills, and inevitably draws the participant closer to God.

Eighth Blessing: Temple Ordinances

An important aspect of the Latter-day Saint experience is to go into the temple to perform sacred ordinance work, either for yourself or vicariously for others. Each person preparing to go to the temple is required to have a recommend, which can be obtained after a private interview with a member of the ward bishopric and then with a member of the stake presidency. These priesthood leaders will ask a specific set of questions to ascertain the member's personal worthiness. These will include questions about tithing, loyalty to the Church and its leaders, moral cleanliness, obedience to the Word of Wisdom, living the lifestyle of a Saint in Sunday activities, affiliation with any questionable society, and honorable dealings with family members and others. If the member is found worthy, the recommend is signed by the bishop and the stake presidency member. Considerable importance is placed on the individual's own signature to attest worthiness. Anyone going to the temple to do ordinance work must show his or her recommend at the temple entrance. It is nontransferable and must be renewed through the same process annually.

Temple blessings are personal and kept strictly sacred. Several different ordinances are performed inside the temple for the living and also vicariously for those who have died without the benefit of these necessary ordinances. The temple is for adults, married or single, who are spiritually prepared and who are recommended by their bishop as worthy and needful of taking the next important step in preparing for eternity. (It is worth noting here that certain temple ordinances can involve those who are not yet adults. The sealing of children to parents is one; baptisms for the dead is another. Young baptized members of the Church who are twelve years of age or older may obtain a recommend from the bishop to go to the temple to participate in baptisms for the dead.)

Because of the personal preparation of those who enter the temple to enjoy the sacred gospel principles taught there, the Holy Ghost can bless those in attendance richly. Many marvelous things occur that simply do not happen outside the temples themselves. After formal dedication ceremonies, Latter-day Saint temples are not open to public perusal or used for regular worship services. They are busy places where certain of the Lord's revealed ordinances are performed. Precious privileges established by God for the progress of his children are received there and are preparatory for exaltation after death.

Every new member of the Church is encouraged to prepare to go to the temple. Usually this takes about a year's effort to prepare personally and make proper arrangements, such as receiving a recommend. Many Church units conduct temple preparation classes.

Ninth Blessing: "By the Laying on of Hands"

The ideal is for every family to be complete with a member of the priesthood, someone who can perform certain ordinances and provide certain blessings to family members. He often asks another priesthood member to assist. If there is no father in the home or if the person in the family holding the priesthood is unavailable or unworthy, the family may readily call upon the ward structure to provide such experiences that come by "the laying on of hands."

This is one wonderful way that people give loving service to each other in The Church of Jesus Christ of Latter-day Saints.

Following is a list of blessings that can be given through the Melchizedek Priesthood, along with a description of each and an explanation of who may perform it.

Father's Blessing

A father who holds the Melchizedek Priesthood is entitled, and expected, to take his newborn baby and give it a name and a father's blessing. In this blessing, he expresses what the Spirit directs regarding this precious little person in the family, including blessings that he or she might enjoy throughout his or her life. Help can also come through the priesthood quorum and worthy male family members.

A father is also entitled to lay his hands upon the heads of his family members or friends upon request to bless them as they prepare for marriage, school, or a new job; to give them strength to change their life course; or to comfort and receive protection in times when the family is to be separated for a period.

A poignant record of a father's blessing is found in Genesis, chapter 49. It follows the tender, thought-provoking reunion in Egypt of Joseph and his father and brothers. Father Jacob is 110 years old when he blesses his sons. Each son, a head of a tribe, learns what the Lord and life has in store for him. The record says, "And when Jacob had made an end of commanding his sons, he gathered up his feet into the bed, and yielded up the ghost, and was gathered unto his people" (Genesis 49:33).

Jacob's giving a father's blessing to his children is an appropriate example for any Latter-day Saint father to follow. Sometimes it takes a mother to do the prodding and reminding or a child to request it, but great are the rewards of giving and receiving such blessings. I know personally of several moving incidents among my own associates where blessings given by a father one last time have truly changed lives!

Healing Blessing

A person who is sick or otherwise afflicted may request holders of the Melchizedek Priesthood to administer to them; that is, give them a blessing of comfort or healing. This is usually done by two priesthood holders: first, one will anoint the head of the person receiving the blessing with consecrated oil; then both will lay their hands on the person's head, and the second priesthood holder will "seal the anointing" and say those things that he receives through inspiration, which is understood to be the Lord's will for the person in these circumstances and at this time.

Coke Newell's story of an experience he, as a relatively new member of the Church, had with the priesthood is a choice perspective about the blessings of membership. He writes:

> "I have what is called the priesthood," I quietly told my friend Maria Torres. Blankets hung over every window, and the house was dark and gloomy, as if the inhabitants were retreating from the cold of winter and sorrow.
>
> "With it I can give blessings, like in the New Testament," I said. And with enough faith, I thought, people can be healed. Do I have enough faith, I wondered?
>
> I had been a member of the Church for a year and had just been ordained an elder a few weeks before I returned home to my small town in Colorado for the Christmas holiday. I wasn't completely familiar with Church procedures, but I knew about the priesthood and had seen its power manifest. I had met Maria before I left for college. She had encouraged me to overcome my life-long fear of water and had taught me how to swim. Now it was my turn to offer help.
>
> Her husband had just walked out of her life, leaving her with bills, no job, and two children under the age of four. Maria's sister had arrived on a bus from California the night before to offer comfort and assistance. Now both of Maria's children were sick.
>
> "Do you have faith in the Savior?" I asked Maria.
>
> She said she did.
>
> "Would you like me to give you a blessing?"
>
> Again, the answer was yes.
>
> I was frightened and a bit awkward as I laid my hands on her head and searched my mind and heart for the proper words to say in the first blessing I had ever given as an elder.
>
> When I finished, Maria took me into her four-year-old son's room, asking me to give him a "prayer," too. Next I was asked to

bless the baby, and then Maria's sister placed a chair in front of me and sat down, bowing her head. She wanted to be next.

After giving the blessings, as I walked out of the house and approached my beat-up Volkswagen, I thought of my inexperience. But then a beautiful feeling overwhelmed me, and the tears I had been holding back flooded into my eyes.

I knew then that my friends would recover their health and reassemble their lives. Their faith would grow, and perhaps even lead them to the Savior, as it had me.

And I realized that by receiving the priesthood, I had received a blessing that would stay with me forever. (Coke Newell, "I Can Give Blessings," *Ensign*, August 1993, p. 58. © The Church of Jesus Christ of Latter-day Saints. Used by permission.)

May *you* always be God-blessed! And may you remember the power implicit in the words of the Lord, "Be still and know that I am God"! (Doctrine and Covenants 101:16.)

Patriarchal Blessing

This is the only blessing that is recorded and placed on file in the Church archives by the stake patriarch. Although it contains certain standard elements—such as a declaration of lineage in the house of Israel—the language, promises, and counsel are unique for the individual.

All official Church action taken with an individual member is a matter of record in the archives of The Church of Jesus Christ of Latter-day Saints, including certificates of baptism, confirmation, priesthood ordination, temple endowment and marriage. A transcript of a member's patriarchal blessing becomes a part of those official files.

A candidate for a patriarchal blessing must be of sufficient age and spiritual development to appreciate the personal guidance. During the early teen years or at the time of some major event—such as leaving home for missionary service, school, or marriage—are often the times a person feels the desire for such a blessing. My own father was given his patriarchal blessing when he was many times a grandfather! It was a great comfort to him, however, because he died knowing his lineage in the house of Israel and feeling comforted that the Lord did have things to be said especially to him. He treasured that experience to his grave.

To receive such a blessing, you must have an interview with your bishop. If he feels you are ready, he will give you a special recommend. You can then make an appointment with the stake patriarch. Prepare yourself spiritually to go before the Lord and receive what he has to say to you personally. Your lineage will be declared—that is, which tribe of Israel is your heritage. Sacred, wonderful promises are often expressed, and the patriarch will give you the counsel for your entire life that the Spirit reveals to him. The fulfillment of patriarchal blessings, like those given in temple ordinance work, are dependent upon your continued faithfulness and upon their being sealed by the Holy Spirit of Promise.

When you have your patriarchal blessing, it is a personal matter. It is not necessary for anyone to accompany you to the appointment, but if you are still living with your parents you might want to have them accompany you. You will receive a transcription of the blessing given to you, which you will want to keep sacred and secure. Refer to it often for inspiration, guidance, and a reminder of the importance of qualifying for such incredible promises from God.

Tenth Blessing: The Worth of Souls

Church membership opens new vistas to the nature of God. All honest religions teach of a higher power, but only The Church of Jesus Christ of Latter-day Saints has the correct details about God's nature and the worth of souls to him. We know not only that he lives and cares about us but also that we are precious to him. His life's work is about us—to bring to pass our immortality and eternal life (see Moses 1:39). Our Heavenly Father is creator and author of the plan whereby we may attain exaltation, not just resurrection, wonderful though that may be, and which we may enjoy because of the atonement of Christ.

The gospel promotes respect for each individual; hence our programs of proselyting and redeeming the individual! Having the fulness of the truth in this church increases our understanding. The worth of souls is understood better, and our interaction with God and with each other is sweeter. Your views, talents, and needs are valid. All of God's children across the nations and around the world were with him in the premortal life and have the potential to return to live with him. This church shows God's way for us to make that return safely. You can have confidence in the order of it all—the marvelous system built on irrevocable divine laws, consequences, continuity of effort, and personal progression.

Blessings Untold: Rewards in Membership

There are some additional things to think about—blessings to count—that add luster, joy, purpose, and success to your own life just because you are a member of the Lord's church on earth at this time, just because you try each day to live more completely after the manner of happiness he has defined. Count your many blessings—untold and unimagined outpourings from heaven.

Remember in your life, God is in the details! You can be deeply grateful for—

- A personal testimony. This is a sure witness given to you through the power of the Holy Ghost—a feeling that you cannot describe easily but neither can you doubt—that Christ lives, loves you, and *knows* you! It assures you that you can believe what Christ says.
- The miracle of drawing on the powers of heaven to bless you and those you love. This is a whole gamut of wonders that unfold as you are ready to receive them.
- The anticipation of Sunday, its richness, and its preparation for the new week ahead.
- The hope of eternal life.
- The friends who surround you, the doors that have opened, the doubts that have been dispelled just because of the doctrine and structure of this inspired church you have joined. It just makes a difference!

As you kneel in prayer and report to God at the end of each day, you will feel a gentle peace. Since your acceptance of this new lifestyle, this God-given plan of life, you have so much to be grateful for, including strength to resist old habits, temptations, and confusions. When you actually live by the will of the Lord and obey his word, you come to know the source of your strength!

You are expected to be a lively member, to be anxiously engaged in the good cause and grand opportunities the Church provides. Be first to smile, first to speak, first to offer a hand and to make introductions. Get in there and circulate. Be patient with others who haven't learned this yet, and help all you can. Your entire Church experience— religious worship and service—will benefit as you continue to grow and understand more. Seek Jesus always. At the center of your mind and heart, put his name, his mission, his redeeming love for you.

Again, I pray that you may always be God-blessed! May you remember the power implicit in the words of the Lord, "Be still and know that I am God" (Doctrine and Covenants 101:16).

6

Making the Ideal Real

The goal of the Christian who is also a Latter-day Saint is grander than the evangelical echo, "I accept Christ" or "I believe!"

Beyond belief is personal change. Faith in Christ is active, not passive. It is ongoing. We believe that we should become as much like Jesus Christ as we possibly can in this life, for the Lord asked, "Therefore, what manner of men [and women] ought ye to be?" Then he answered his own question, "Verily I say unto you, even as I am." (3 Nephi 27:27.)

This is the ideal.

Making the ideal real is another matter.

Of course, we couldn't have a more noble role model. Jesus is our Creator. He knows heaven and he knows us. His example and our living by eternal principles can bring us together.

Beyond Sunday rituals is the daily application in life of eternal gospel principles. This is the way change in us occurs. Saying so doesn't make it so, but here are five winning steps to consider:

1. *Recognize the need to change.* Compare yourself to Jesus Christ, our example. Make a checklist of those personal areas where change will benefit you.

2. *Put yourself in a position to change.* A person needing to lose weight will probably have a harder time working in a sweet shop. You

have taken the first step in spiritual change by becoming part of the Church of Jesus Christ and placing yourself close to him.

3. *Seek information you can act upon.* Make full use of the God-given principles taught in Christ's system for success. Note the marvelous rewards for progress. Search the scriptures and listen to the prophet's voice.

4. *Apply the new information to your life.* Consider the difference between being merely convinced and truly converted. People know what puts weight on the body, but unless they actually experience the success of changing their eating habits, losing weight, and feeling better, it is as if for them the truth doesn't exist! Living the gospel proves its benefits (see John 7:17).

5. *Accept motivating support.* The people of this Church want you to succeed. It is their underlying mission to help you—let them! God has put the saving principles and ordinances in place, along with incentives to qualify for further spiritual growth. Checkpoints such as personal interviews, membership tracking, and fellowshipping help to motivate and support you. The Lord wants you to succeed most of all. He is gracious and merciful. He has ways to be miraculously supportive.

The Inevitable Discouragement

I have always taken great comfort in the incident recorded in Mark 9:17–27. A grieved father brought his critically ill son to be blessed by Jesus: "I have brought unto thee my son, which hath a dumb spirit; . . . he . . . gnashed with his teeth, and pineth away." In the presence of Jesus, the boy "fell on the ground, and wallowed foaming"!

The father pleaded, "If thou canst do any thing, have compassion on us, and help us."

Jesus replied, "If thou canst believe, all things are possible to him that believeth."

Perhaps the man worried that the possibility of the boy's healing depended upon himself, for he cried out with tears, "Lord, I believe; help thou mine unbelief." (Here is the cry of every needful being: "I believe, but Lord, *help thou my unbelief!*")

Jesus took the boy by the hand, the scriptures tell us, "and lifted him up; and he arose."

Incredible! Wonderful! And he will lift us in our need.

Change is ongoing for members of the Church. You should constantly upgrade your goals as you increase in spiritual understanding. Remember, eternal principles are God's principles. These principles never change, and they always work to our benefit. The creator of us all has supplied these instructions as a type of "owner's operating manual" to help us live on earth in a productive, purifying way.

In mortality, Jesus lived according to eternal principles, and he continues to do so now. He is our example. His teachings abound with incidents and instruction proving the value of these principles and his life.

Jesus Grew Spiritually and Physically

As a youth, Jesus learned and waxed strong, physically and spiritually. By the age of twelve, he confidently shared what he already knew! Do you recall the impressive story recorded in Luke of Christ teaching the wise men at the temple? When Jesus was twelve years old, his parents had been looking for him. "And it came to pass, that after three days they found him in the temple, sitting in the midst of the doctors, both hearing them, and asking them questions. And all that heard him were astonished at his understanding and answers." (Luke 2:46–47.)

As you begin to learn the gospel principles, to live by them and to share them, your relationships with God and others will be more rewarding. "Jesus increased in wisdom and stature, and in favour with God and man" (Luke 2:52). *So can you. Your walk among people will be like a blessing from heaven.*

Jesus Prepared to Serve God

Jesus prepared himself to effectively bring people to God. He sought out John the Baptist and was baptized by immersion and apparently also confirmed. The Holy Ghost descended on him, symbolized by "a bodily shape like a dove." The voice of God declared who Jesus really was: "Thou art my beloved Son; in thee I am well pleased." (Luke 3:21–22.) Similarly, baptism, confirmation, and the gift of the Holy Ghost are necessary for your own service to others in the name of God.

When Jesus was about thirty years old, "being full of the Holy Ghost" he was led by the Spirit into the wilderness, where he spent forty days. During this time he was tempted by the devil, and he overcame the temptations. He fasted, and the record explains that when he had finished the fast he hungered. (See Luke 4:1–13.)

When we set our minds to fast for spiritual strength, guidance, and closeness to the Lord, our own experience will be similar to Christ's. Angels attended him. We too are entitled to such help!

Jesus Outlined His Mission

Jesus went to the synagogue one Sabbath day, and "the eyes of all them that were in the synagogue were fastened on him" as he read his life's purposes from the scriptures (see Luke 4:16–20):

- to preach the gospel to the poor
- to heal the brokenhearted
- to preach deliverance to the captives
- to preach recovering of sight to the blind
- to set at liberty them that are bruised

The more closely your personal goals and purpose reflect Christ in your life, the more effective you'll be in making the ideal real.

His Word Was Power

Because of his preparation to serve, Jesus was filled with the Spirit. His fame went out round about as he healed the sick, the lame, and the lepers; raised the dead; and delivered the devils out of many.

You have the promise from God that in your own way, in your own time, you too can serve others in an incredibly marvelous way. If you are filled with the Spirit of God, if you live in increasing purity, you can become ever more like Jesus.

Jesus Was What He Taught

Jesus taught people to rejoice in serving and to "leap for joy" in the goodness of God (Luke 6:23). He taught us to trust in God and be at peace. It was he who slept in peace when the storms came and put the ship in jeopardy. Another time, he walked on the water and helped Peter to do the same until Peter's faith wavered.

Whatever his will is for you will be all right; he is the wisest and most loving of beings. You can follow his example of faith unto peace.

Jesus taught that we should love our enemies and pray for those who despitefully use us, even turning the other cheek. This is tough to do sometimes, but again we look to our prime example and take comfort that God will help us. And we keep on trying, repenting, praying for help, and trying again.

Jesus prayed for the Roman soldiers who crucified him and pled with the Father to forgive them, for they did not know what they were doing! Jesus is our advocate as well.

Jesus taught that it wasn't enough to praise him as Lord, but we must also follow the things he taught (see Matthew 7:21).

The Church of Jesus Christ of Latter-day Saints and its devoted members do not give mere lip service to the Lord, nor is the gospel only for Sunday worship.

To follow Christ is to live each day by his teachings. The covenants you made with him at baptism and those you make during the sacrament each Sunday are tied directly to becoming his disciple in all you do.

Jesus used the example of Mary and Martha to teach values—what really is important. He said to the complaining Martha, who was cumbered with much serving, "Martha, Martha, thou art careful and troubled about many things: but one thing is needful: and Mary hath chosen that good part, which shall not be taken away from her" (Luke 10:41–42).

For Jesus the valuable thing was enrichment of the soul through spiritual growth, as Mary had shown by sitting at the feet of Jesus while he taught her. This is the lesson for you!

Godly Counsel

The following suggestions are time and people tested. They are gospel based. They can be helpful in your quest to follow the example of Jesus and make the ideal real:

1. *Experiment upon the word.* Try the commandments of God. This is the counsel that Alma gave the Zoramites (see Alma 32). He likened

the word of God unto a seed. He told the people to plant the seed and watch it flourish. If it didn't grow, they should not understand this to mean the seed wasn't good. Rather, it could not grow, because their "ground [was] barren" and could not nourish the tree of life that the seed should become. Alma's counsel is as true today as it ever was:

> If ye will nourish the word, yea, nourish the tree as it beginneth to grow, by your faith with great diligence, and with patience, looking forward to the fruit thereof, it shall take root; and behold it shall be a tree springing up unto everlasting life.
>
>   . . . Ye shall pluck the fruit thereof, which is most precious, which is sweet above all that is sweet, . . . and ye shall feast upon this fruit even until ye are filled, that ye hunger not, neither shall ye thirst." (Alma 32:41–42.)

2. *Save yourself from error.* In most circles, ignorance of the law will not prevent you from paying the consequences of breaking the law. Ignorance of the law can also deprive you from the blessing the law governs. It works two ways.

First, learn God's laws. They do not change and are a means of educating people for the eternal life God has in store for his children. If you want the blessing, you must know the law and live that law that governs the blessing. The Lord explains it this way: "There is a law, irrevocably decreed in heaven before the foundations of this world, upon which all blessings are predicated—and when we obtain any blessing from God, it is by obedience to that law upon which it is predicated" (Doctrine and Covenants 130:20–21).

Second, it is important to learn how to judge good from evil, right from wrong, wise from foolish so that you can make correct choices for you. The Lord has given you a yardstick or a measuring rod by which to judge what is worthwhile and true and what isn't:

> The Spirit of Christ is given to every man, that he may know good from evil; wherefore, I show unto you the way to judge; for every thing which inviteth to do good, and to persuade to believe in Christ, is sent forth by the power and gift of Christ; wherefore ye may know with a perfect knowledge it is of God.
>
>   But whatsoever thing persuadeth men to do evil, and believe not in Christ, and deny him, and serve not God, then ye may

know with a perfect knowledge it is of the devil; for after this manner doth the devil work, for he persuadeth no man to do good, no, not one; neither do his angels; neither do they who subject themselves unto him. (Moroni 7:16–17.)

3. *Love one another.* The gospel principles and Church programs are based on the premise that today is part of eternity and that love makes the mellow difference. You have many options to serve, to comfort, to offer relief, to lift spirits, to inspire, and to give further light and knowledge to others. There are methods to keep track of each other and ways for the lost sheep to be helped, rescued, and returned to the safety of the flock. You are called to be blessed by the effective procedures and true principles for the success of this work found in The Church of Jesus Christ of Latter-day Saints.

4. *Lay hold on every good thing.* The prophet Mormon taught that all good things come from Christ (Moroni 7:24–26):

- "All things which are good cometh of Christ."
- "By the ministering of angels, and by every word which [proceedeth] forth out of the mouth of God, men [begin] to exercise faith in Christ."
- "Lay hold upon every good thing."
- "[Christ] spake these words . . . , saying: Whatsoever thing ye shall ask the Father in my name, which is good, in faith believing that ye shall receive, behold, it shall be done unto you."

That scripture is such a remarkable promise that some newcomers to the Church who discover it want to print it in giant letters and secure it in a most visible spot as a constant reminder.

The abundant life that Church membership offers you is life according to the will of Christ, with grace upon grace unfolding as you are ready to receive it. There is always something more to learn, some fresh joy to experience. There is also the promise that we can become like Him, if we put our foot to the path and then keep on moving in the right direction.

7

The Inspired Church Structure

Not only is the gospel of Jesus Christ true for Latter-day Saints but so also is the institution that governs its physical manifestation. Its very structure was inspired by God to ensure success in its mission of inviting all to "come unto Christ" (Moroni 10:32) through preaching the gospel, redeeming the dead, and helping the members ever move forward in personal progress toward perfection.

Many of you may not have heard of the Church or its members before you met the missionaries who brought you its message. Others of you may have married a member of the Church; or your child became converted because friends shared their testimonies; or you bunked in the military with someone who was a practicing Latter-day Saint. Perhaps you came to the Church because of your own struggling spirit—a kind of holy restlessness that put you searching for truth from God and for answers to life's big questions. You prayed for help and it came!

My own story is that I was born into an LDS family, in the covenant as we say. I was trained up by parents who believed in the admonition of Proverbs 22:6: "Train up a child in the way he should go: and when he is old, he will not depart from it." In college I chose to learn it all again for myself, this time through my own study. In time I tested each principle and tradition that I could against the rigid marker of revealed truth. I learned by study in campus courses of comparative religion and by lecture at the Church institute of religion. I learned by faithfully and prayerfully seeking knowledge in the standard works of the Church. It has been a fascinating experience to learn the link between God and his children since the beginning of time. I know that this church is patterned by God and is eternally tied to ancient "saving remnants" of his covenant children. It is true. Through the power of the Holy Ghost, my search for truth has been rewarded and confirmed. This church is true. My extensive participation in the Church programs and ordinances for personal enhancement has proven to be a mighty blessing in my life. The structure of the Church itself is marvelous and a remarkable evidence of God's hand. It is sufficient for the whole Christian philosophy and plan of salvation it espouses.

The True Church

What kind of institution is this church that has now taken such a sweet hold on your life? What makes the LDS church different from the last group you worshiped with? How is it governed and how is it structured to include *you*? How does this church allow individual growth and provide rich spiritual development?

Not only was the Church of Jesus Christ established by the Lord Jesus Christ, it is also directed by him through his prophets and other authorized servants on earth.

Joseph Smith learned about other churches when he was fourteen years old. He prayed about which church to join. You can read about this for yourself in Joseph Smith—History 1:7–20. Several years later, after God's true church had been organized on earth again, Jesus told Joseph Smith that the church he had established under divine direction was "the only true and living church upon the face of the whole earth, with which I, the Lord, am well pleased, speaking unto the church collectively and not individually" (Doctrine and Covenants 1:30). This church was brought out of obscurity, according to the Lord, so that men would not be dependent upon only the wisdom of other men for their religious understanding. The Church of Jesus Christ was established so that—

- The fulness of the gospel might be available to all mankind.
- Faith might increase on the earth.
- God's everlasting covenant might be established.
- Humble people might be made strong.
- Continuous revelation could bless the lives of members.
- Sinners might be chastened, repent, and learn God's will for them.

A stunning reminder of where this doctrine comes from lies in this powerful statement, "Behold, I am God and have spoken it" (Doctrine and Covenants 1:24).

These factors of the true Church impact positively and inevitably upon each member's life and his or her ability to cope in daily life while trying to properly prepare for eternal life. Surely it is important for God's church that people are enabled to effectively grow ever closer to the Lord and to feel at peace.

Member Participation

Leadership, service, and meaningful activities are some of the benefits for you in the LDS church.

The Church has been cited as the most successful volunteer organization in the world. Members on every level of service are frequently asked, "How do you do it? How do you get people to fill missions at their own expense, teach lessons and keep up with a heavy schedule of Church activity, pay a full tithing monthly, sing in choirs, and engage in projects and programs without pay?"

The answer is implicit in our deep spiritual conviction and in our personal growth we enjoy by serving in the Church system. We believe that in doing these things—in serving others—we are serving God and furthering the work of the kingdom of God on earth. At baptism we covenanted with him to do just that.

This church is a church of lay service. In congregations of Latter-day Saints, people serve voluntarily and without remuneration when called to do so by those in authority.

The very structure of the Church for learning, teaching, and doing provides a variety of options for members to serve. People may hold many different assignments in their life of Church service. For example, a man may serve as a bishop of a ward, and when he is released from that calling he could be assigned or called by the new bishop to be the Scout leader or a Sunday School teacher. A woman might serve as general president of the Relief Society for the worldwide Church, and upon her release she may be called by her local bishop to teach Gospel Doctrine lessons to adults or help with name extraction in the Church's family history program.

You will have the opportunity to serve in a position for a time and then be released so another may have that opportunity to serve, learn, and grow. There is no definite time period for any local Church assignment.

The Mission of the Church

The mission of the Church is to "invite all to come unto Christ" (Doctrine and Covenants 20:59) "and be perfected in him" (Moroni 10:32). This mission has three general areas of responsibility:

- To proclaim the gospel of the Lord Jesus Christ to every nation, kindred, tongue, and people.
- To perfect the Saints by preparing them to receive the ordinances of the gospel for exaltation.
- To redeem the dead by performing vicarious ordinances of the gospel for those who have lived on the earth.

The historical and contemporary structure and workings of Christ's church are inextricably meshed with God's eternal plan for man. The mission of Jesus Christ, as he himself has stated, is "to bring to pass the immortality and eternal life of man" (Moses 1:39).

Faithful Church members are involved in the Church for the express purpose of helping Christ in his mission. This is what the Church is structured to do on the general, local, and individual levels.

People could be witnesses of Christ in their lives; they could do good deeds and live strict moral standards; they could praise God and accept his grace—they could do all this and more and yet not be involved in any formal church. On the other hand, The Church of Jesus Christ of Latter-day Saints offers direction for a way of life with the purpose of getting oneself—and also helping others—through earthly experiences by doing the Lord's will and participating in his saving ordinances.

This can only happen in a church with an inspired structure, with leaders who are authorized by God to do the work and who receive continuing revelation to guide each of us in that work.

The Authority from God

The priesthood is both the organizing and the operating authority of the Church; priesthood keys and authority come from God. The President of the Church is the only person on earth who has the authority from God at any one time to hold all the keys to the fulness of the gospel experience for us and for the accomplishment of each phase of His work.

The President of the Church delegates different keys or assignments for sacred, saving work to individuals who have been called, ordained, or set apart for specific responsibilities. This is not, of course, done by whim or circumstance. This system is a strict hierarchy with Christ at its head, as was the case in the ancient Church. Today's Church is governed just as Paul described in his day: "Now therefore ye are no more strangers and foreigners, but fellow citizens with the saints, and of the household of God; and are built upon the foundation of the apostles and prophets, Jesus Christ himself being the chief corner stone" (Ephesians 2:19–20).

Two Priesthoods

It is important to remember that in the Church are two priesthoods, the Melchizedek Priesthood and the Aaronic Priesthood. "The Melchizedek Priesthood holds the right of presidency, and has power and authority over all the offices in the church in all ages of the world" (Doctrine and Covenants 107:8). The power of the priesthood has been given "for the last days and for the last time, in the which is the dispensation of the fulness of times" (Doctrine and Covenants 112:30).

Presidencies, Quorums, Councils

The Church government is priesthood directed and led, and is made up of presidencies, priesthood quorums, and councils. The presidencies, priesthood quorums, and councils exist on the general, stake, and ward levels. The president of an organization has the keys to lead and make decisions for the stewardship or office he holds. Others may counsel with the president, vote, accept assignments, and contribute perspective and good ideas. In the case of a ward, the bishop serves as president of the Aaronic Priesthood, presiding high priest, and shepherd of the ward congregation.

Women and the Priesthood

Women in the Church are not ordained to a priesthood office. It is not their God-given role. However, women serve as representatives on certain Church committees, councils, and boards at the general, stake, and ward levels. Women compose the presidencies of the Relief Society, Young Women, and Primary organizations. They also fill responsibilities in the Sunday School organization and serve on committees in areas such as activities, welfare, family history, and missionary service.

God-given Roles

Latter-day Saints believe that the spirit in a person has been male or female since the beginning (see Doctrine and Covenants 77:2; *Encyclopedia of Mormonism* ed. Daniel H. Ludlow, 5 vols. [New York: Macmillan, 1992], 3:1404–5). Legislation, restlessness, or any other form of worldly power will not change this. The order that God speaks of as being in his house includes the assignments or roles that males and females are given both generally and specifically. In The Church of Jesus Christ of Latter-day Saints, this order is reflected in the inspired structure of the Church.

To the men God has given to lead, govern, and preside in Church government and as head of the family. This provides that there may be order rather than confusion in the Church and in the home and that people may learn to honor authority. Priesthood bearers are to love, cherish, provide for, and protect their precious family members. Like other Church members, they are expected to love their fellowmen and particularly to love and serve other Church members in their particular sphere of assignment.

To the women God has given to be his particular agents for

compassionate service—to spread love, nurture, give birth to and rear babies, and comfort the needy. They are encouraged to become educated and to polish their skills for effective service, homemaking, financial management, crisis survival, and negotiating relationships.

God requires both male and female members of the Church of all ages to learn the gospel so that they may live it and obey his commandments. All members also need to participate in the saving ordinances found only in the Church of Jesus Christ. They are urged to be valiant and continue to grow and spiritually mature, becoming ever more like their beloved Example, Jesus Christ, until their time on earth is finished. In these things there is no difference between a man and a woman.

But in the role of prime assignment, there are clear-cut, God-given, unchangeable responsibilities. Each shares and assists the other. A man is not without the woman in the highest degree of glory. A woman does not conceive children on her own. This great blending of purpose and power matches the wise clarification of the role each primarily plays.

So That All May Be Blessed

When a boy turns twelve in the Church, he begins his life of service in the priesthood of God on earth. Different priesthood callings, or power and authority to serve in a special way, are given him along the path of his life. Ideally, every faithful Latter-day Saint boy and man will progress in activity and receive the highest, or Melchizedek, priesthood.

When a girl becomes a young woman about the age of twelve, her body changes and becomes ready for her role as mother. She doesn't have to go through certain lessons—such as diapering, feeding, or guarding an infant—before she can become a mother. However, the Church does provide certain training that can help. Chastity before marriage and fidelity within marriage is extensively taught. Training in how to nurture others is given in the women's organizations. Though she may actually never bear children, a woman can still be an influence for good. Her mission as a daughter of God is glorious.

When a boy turns twelve, he is interviewed by his bishop. If he is found worthy, he is sustained by the ward congregation and then, by the laying on of hands, is ordained as a deacon in the Aaronic, or lesser, Priesthood. He is given the responsibility to pass the sacrament and assist in the collection of fast offerings.

When he turns fourteen, the boy is again interviewed for personal worthiness by his bishop. If he qualifies, his name is presented to the congregation, and he is sustained and later ordained as a teacher in the Aaronic Priesthood. Additional assignments are then given to him to prepare the sacrament and serve as a home teacher.

At age sixteen, the worthy young man follows the same pattern. He is interviewed, sustained, and ordained a priest. He is given additional authority. He now can administer the sacrament by offering the sacramental prayers, as well as being able to prepare and pass the sacrament. He also has the authority to baptize, though confirmation and bestowal of the gift of the Holy Ghost is a function of those holding the Melchizedek Priesthood. The priest now formally prepares himself to serve a mission when he turns nineteen, at which point, or a little earlier, he is ordained an elder in the Melchizedek Priesthood.

This higher priesthood incorporates several offices. A bearer of this priesthood has many opportunities to use the delegated power of God to bring health, joy, comfort, and progress to Heavenly Father's children who desire this help. With this higher priesthood, he may now confirm people as members of the Church; anoint and seal the anointing in a healing blessing; give a name and a blessing to a baby; and, when so called, serve in quorum presidencies and on committees, and as a bishop, stake presidency member, or General Authority of the Church.

It is good for women, men, and children to understand these priesthood functions.

Common Consent

A prominent feature of the priesthood governing system is the law of common consent. Any person selected to serve in a Church assignment must receive a formal sustaining vote from the membership he or she will serve. This sustaining vote given by each member commits the member's support to the leaders in their work of the kingdom.

A System of Order

There is order in the Lord's church. All administrations, offices, meetings, callings to service and subsequent release, ordinances, record keeping, and finances—as well as exercising Church discipline and the restoration of blessings—proceed as defined by revelation and according to instructions in the *General Handbook of Instructions* for Melchizedek Priesthood leaders.

The Church today is built upon Apostles and prophets; Jesus is indeed the chief cornerstone. If a man is absent from a governing council because of illness, travel, or causes incident to old age (and God has not released him from service), the affairs of the Church roll forward.

The President of the Church

The President of the Church is the presiding high priest, Apostle, and prophet, a position he occupies until his death. He serves the Lord, the Church system and membership, and all people. Whoever he is, he is loved and valued, but not worshiped. He is the first to witness that Christ is the head of the Church!

The Church is governed by quorums, not people. When people die, move, or simply fail to do their duty, the work of the ward, stake, or whole Church goes forward uninterrupted because of the inspired genius of the structure.

When Joseph Smith and his brother Hyrum were martyred, many thought that the Latter-day Saints would scatter in disarray. But the Lord raised up another prophet, Brigham Young, who led the exodus of Saints west. And after President Brigham Young's death, another became prophet and President. So has proceeded the great leadership we have known in these latter days.

Other God-serving men have been called to the leading quorums over the years, even as Matthias was after Judas fell because he betrayed Christ. Thus the work and mission of the Church is carried on by the humble disciples of Christ in each generation. These General Authorities are called from the ranks of membership and leadership on local levels as their contribution is needed. They give up private lives and professional success, leaving the world behind them to devote full time and heart, might, mind, and strength to the work of the Lord in whatever assignments come to them.

Usually—except when on assignment—they live with their families in their own homes in or near Salt Lake City, Utah, and work in Church headquarters in the Great Salt Lake Valley. As well as participating in the daily challenge of moving a powerful church forward, they travel widely, speak and teach almost constantly, administer blessings, and counsel with local leadership.

All of my life I have been blessed to live, work, and rear my family near the headquarters of the Church. Since I was a child, I have known five Presidents of the Church—five prophets of God—well enough that they called me by my first name! This has been a blessing of great worth, for I can witness of the holiness of their calling. I know for myself, in my heart, that each was appointed by God.

During each of the semiannual general conferences held in the Tabernacle on Temple Square, these Brethren give inspired counsel to the Church membership and to countless friends and investigators. The stories of their own sacrifices are as moving as their testimonies of joy in the work and in being special witnesses that Jesus is the Christ. They know that He lives and operates in the affairs of this church.

Church Government

The escalating numbers of members and the success of the Church institution itself attest to the success of the Church system. Quality of life and inner strength are clearly evident among most members. Millions of converts to Christ are joining the Church, including in the far corners of the earth, who then joyfully take up the lifestyle and the disciplines, the service and the commandments.

The highest governing body in the Church is the First Presidency. At the head of the First Presidency is the President and prophet of The Church of Jesus Christ of Latter-day Saints. He holds all the keys of the priesthood for the work of the Lord on earth today. He is the senior Apostle in years of service, as well. The President chooses two counselors to work with him.

The Apostles serve in the Quorum of the Twelve Apostles. The President of that quorum is the senior member based on time of ordination to the apostleship. He is second in seniority to the President of the Church. When the President of the Church dies, his Counselors are released. The Quorum of the Twelve Apostles then is the governing body of the Church until a new President is in place and a new First Presidency organized.

Usually each week, these two presiding quorums meet together as the Council of the First Presidency and the Quorum of the Twelve Apostles. This council decides matters relating to Church policies and administration. (See *Encyclopedia of Mormonism* 1:327.)

But there is more! The people who fill these presiding quorums are warmhearted, devoted disciples of the Lord Jesus Christ. They are willing to immediately shift gears from years in the marketplace to covenant in the holy temple to full-time service in building God's kingdom.

They are, to my personal knowledge, among the finest men I have met at any time or place. Many I have known as neighbors, coworkers at Church headquarters, leaders in our community, or even members of my own immediate circle of family and friends. Some I knew even before they were called to serve as a General Authority. Without exception, their good qualities are noticeably enhanced after they are ordained. Their human tendencies are subdued. When the mantle of this level of service in the Lord's kingdom falls upon their shoulders, they seem more readily filled with light. The steps they conscientiously take toward perfection become evident. It is interesting to note that their individual personalities, when viewed through the prism of time, seem to be sent forth for a particular purpose. They are examples to the rest of the Church because—though they are not flawless—the way of life they follow is God-blessed. The good they do, each in his own way and own time, cannot be measured by mortal means.

There is yet something else. I have witnessed their growth in wisdom and grace, their unselfish, tireless, total commitment to the work of the Lord and their unconditional love for the people of the Church in all walks of life and positions of service! These ordinary human beings, so to speak, prove extra-ordinary as they become visible servants of God who humbly follow his will in bringing their fellow Church members into position for a better life on earth and eventual exaltation in heaven.

General Officers of the Church

No doubt you will be happy to understand and experience for yourself that The Church of Jesus Christ of Latter-day Saints is for everyone—all of God's children of every age, nationality, condition.

The practical effort of reaching people and helping them learn and grow in their own situation in life is incredible. This consideration is a function of the various auxiliary groups and special committees. On the general (or worldwide) and local (stake, ward, branch) levels, there are Sunday School classes for adults and youth; Relief Society for women; Young Men and Young Women for youth aged twelve to eighteen; and Primary for children. There are activities for missionary work and fellowshipping, family history and genealogical research, temple work, welfare work, and projects to strengthen families.

Each organization in the Church has a presidency composed of a president who chooses two counselors. There are also suitable staff members to teach and to assist with activities, service projects, socials, and cultural events.

While there may be changes in these programs because of rapid growth of the Church in one area or a decline of population in another, the orderly procedure of operation follows the same system, and the curriculum always comes from headquarters under the direction of the General Authorities.

The accompanying organization chart gives a visual aid to understanding the principles of operation and the flow of authority in The Church of Jesus Christ of Latter-day Saints in every town and country! Consider how this divinely directed structure impacts upon your life, your closeness to the Lord, and your abilities to cope in this life, to feel peace, and to qualify for eternal blessings.

Church Organizational Structure

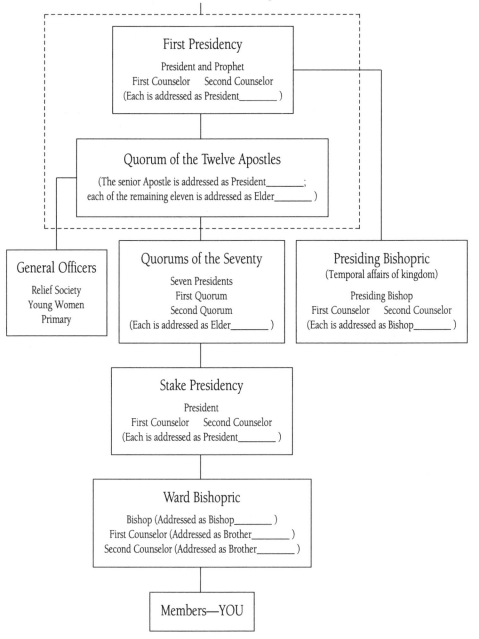

The Council of the First Presidency
and the Quorum of the Twelve Apostles

First Presidency

President and Prophet
First Counselor   Second Counselor
(Each is addressed as President_____)

Quorum of the Twelve Apostles

(The senior Apostle is addressed as President_____;
each of the remaining eleven is addressed as Elder_____)

General Officers

Relief Society
Young Women
Primary

Quorums of the Seventy

Seven Presidents
First Quorum
Second Quorum
(Each is addressed as Elder_____)

Presiding Bishopric
(Temporal affairs of kingdom)

Presiding Bishop
First Counselor   Second Counselor
(Each is addressed as Bishop_____)

Stake Presidency

President
First Counselor   Second Counselor
(Each is addressed as President_____)

Ward Bishopric

Bishop (Addressed as Bishop_____)
First Counselor (Addressed as Brother_____)
Second Counselor (Addressed as Brother_____)

Members—YOU

SECTION TWO

Living by the Gospel's First Principles

8

Come unto Me

Visualize Christ with his arms outstretched toward you, the new convert, as he says, "Welcome! Come unto me!"

How wonderful it would be!

Bertel Thorvaldsen was a nineteenth-century Danish sculptor of international fame. His masterpiece sculpture, *Christus,* depicts the resurrected Christ with his arms outstretched to those who seek truth. Most people are inevitably warmed by this welcoming figure and the concept behind it.

The original of this sculpture stands in the chapel rotunda of an ancient Protestant church in the center of old Copenhagen. An exact replica of this remarkable statue is viewed by thousands weekly as they tour the visitors' center on Temple Square in Salt Lake City, Utah. Some other LDS church information centers have a model of this inspiring statue. While sitting comfortably on cushioned benches, visitors can study the figure of Christ and contemplate the warmth and meaning of his inviting, outstretched arms. The accompanying sound track reminds visitors of the powers of the Creator and the redeeming love of the Savior: "That by him, and through him, and of him, the worlds are and were created, and the inhabitants thereof are begotten sons and daughters unto God" (Doctrine and Covenants 76:24).

There in that dramatic rotunda setting with its star-studded, galaxy-marked background, visitors awaken to new possibilities in life with the help of Christ. And they yearn to live closer to him. It is the inevitable reaction.

Christ does live! Christ *is* there to welcome each of us at any time. Have you noticed that this is true each time you try to live more closely to him and follow his teachings? Each person takes his or her own steps toward the Lord: as the power and the goodness of Christ become evident, you grow stronger in your faith. The gospel does work! There is value in keeping the Lord's commandments. You come to understand that these unchangeable laws he has given us to live by are for the good of all. When you accept the Lord's invitation to come unto him, these words of the Savior, given at one time to Oliver Cowdery, can motivate you to earnestly press forward: "Be faithful and diligent in keeping the commandments of God, and I will encircle thee in the arms of my love" (Doctrine and Covenants 6:20).

Orson F. Whitney was one of the Twelve Apostles in the Church from 1906 to 1931. He wrote his life story under the title *Through Memory's Halls* (Independence, Mo.: Zion's Printing and Publishing Company, 1930). Included is one of Elder Whitney's most remarkable spiritual experiences, which happened when he was a young missionary:

> Then came a marvelous manifestation, and admonition from a higher source, one impossible to ignore. It was a dream, or a vision in a dream, as I lay upon my bed in the little town of Columbia, Lancaster County, Pennsylvania. I seemed to be in the Garden of Gethsemane, a witness of the Savior's agony. I saw Him as plainly as ever I have seen anyone. Standing behind a tree in the foreground, I beheld Jesus, with Peter, James and John, as they came through a little wicket gate at my right. Leaving the three Apostles there, after telling them to kneel and pray, the Son of God passed over to the other side, where He also knelt and prayed. It was the same prayer with which all Bible readers are familiar: "Oh my Father, if it be possible, let this cup pass from me; nevertheless not as I will, but as thou wilt."
>
> As He prayed the tears streamed down His face, which was toward me. I was so moved at the sight that I also wept, out of pure sympathy. My whole heart went out to Him; I loved Him with all my soul, and longed to be with Him as I longed for nothing else.

Presently He arose and walked to where those Apostles were kneeling—fast asleep! He shook them gently, awoke them, and in a tone of tender reproach, untinctured by the least show of anger or impatience, asked them plaintively if they could not watch with Him one hour. There He was, with the awful weight of the world's sin upon His shoulders, with the pangs of every man, woman and child shooting through His sensitive soul—and they could not watch with Him one poor hour!

Returning to His place, He offered up the same prayer as before; then went back and again found them sleeping. Again He awoke them, readmonished them, and once more returned and prayed. Three times this occurred, until I was perfectly familiar with His appearance—face, form and movements. He was of noble stature and majestic mien—not at all the weak, effeminate being that some painters have portrayed; but the very God that He was and is, as meek and humble as a little child.

All at once the circumstance seemed to change, the scene remaining just the same. Instead of before, it was after the crucifixion, and the Savior, with the three Apostles, now stood together in a group at my left. They were about to depart and ascend into Heaven. I could endure it no longer. I ran from behind the tree, fell at His feet, clasped Him around the knees, and begged Him to take me with Him.

I shall never forget the kind and gentle manner in which He stooped, raised me up, and embraced me. It was so vivid, so real. I felt the very warmth of His body, as He held me in His arms and said in tenderest tones: "No, my son; these have finished their work; they can go with me; but you must stay and finish yours." Still I clung to Him. Gazing up into His face—for He was taller than I—I besought Him fervently: "Well, promise me that I will come to you at the last." Smiling sweetly, He said: "That will depend entirely upon yourself." I awoke with a sob in my throat, and it was morning.

"That's from God," said Elder Musser, when I related to him what I had seen and heard. "I do not need to be told that," was my reply. I saw the moral clearly. I had never thought of being an Apostle, nor of holding any other office in the Church, and it did not occur to me even then. Yet I knew that those sleeping Apostles meant me. I was asleep at my post—as any man is who, having been divinely appointed to do one thing, does another.

But from that hour all was changed. I never was the same man again. (Pp. 82–83.)

That all-encompassing, satisfying feeling of being welcomed by the Savior into his presence, of being wrapped in the arms of his love, must be the ultimate emotion. Surely, *then* everything will be all right.

How can you be assured of such a blessing?

You have taken the first step by being baptized and confirmed into Jesus' church as he has commanded (for your own good!). Now you should begin working to bring your spirit into tune with his. Your heart and mind—your very soul—reach out to him as you give thanks, ask for blessings, and try to feel comfortable with him as you pour out your innermost feelings. As you grow in confidence before him, doors open to other remarkable blessings. But "that will depend entirely upon yourself."

Doctrine and Covenants 121:45–46 offers some relevant counsel to apply to your own situation. It is powerful, indeed, to those who have eyes to see and ears to hear and understand the marvelous wonders of eternal life:

Be full of charity towards all men, and to the household of faith, and let virtue garnish thy thoughts unceasingly; *then shall thy confidence wax strong in the presence of God;* and the doctrine of the priesthood shall distil upon thy soul as the dews from heaven.

The Holy Ghost shall be thy constant companion, and thy scepter an unchanging scepter of righteousness and truth; and thy dominion shall be an everlasting dominion, and without compulsory means it shall flow unto thee forever and ever. (Emphasis added.)

Through baptism and confirmation into the LDS church, those converted to Christ have been established as part of the Lord's fold. You have been introduced to a lifestyle of personal growth, of progress to perfection, and of an ever increasing "Christlikeness." You also will come to realize the scope of premortal life, mortality, and the hope and pattern for eternal life. It opens a vision of your own gold chain of relationships from ancestors to descendants.

Jesus was baptized by his cousin John the Baptist. When Jesus came up from the water, a voice came from heaven, saying, "Thou art my beloved Son; in thee I am well pleased" (Luke 3:21–22; see also Matthew 3:13–17).

From this we are comforted that baptism is a family occasion!

Long ago, in the world before this one, each of us was a unique male or female intelligence. Each person who has lived on earth, or ever will, was a spiritually created child of God our Heavenly Father and a Mother in Heaven. You see, Jesus is your Elder Brother. Everybody on earth now and all who ever have been or will be are related in this incredible family circle. This suggests a special bond among your earthly parents, brothers, sisters, friends, teachers, grandparents, children; the missionaries, your bishop, the President of the Church; and even your enemies! You are all brothers and sisters in the family of our Heavenly Father.

We all must keep on growing and learning in this life until we are ready to move forward to another stage. Our loving Elder Brother and those who assist in his work will be there to support, nurture, teach, guide, and nudge you along.

The gospel of Jesus Christ and his restored Church in the latter days provide the blessed opportunity or channel where this experience may best happen to us and where we can help bring about the same joy for others.

It remains now for you to respond to his invitation, "Come unto me."

9

Faith in the Lord Jesus Christ

Faith in the Lord Jesus Christ is the first principle of the gospel. It is common to hear faith spoken of in terms of faith in a scientific procedure, a certain doctor, or a friend or as a desirable quality of character. However, we must develop a different faith—faith in the Lord Jesus Christ. We must pray for and live worthy of this witness through the Holy Ghost, who bears witness of the Father and of the Son. True faith is a gift from God.

Faith is the foundation of all real righteousness, and upon the exercise of your faith hangs your eternal life. Faith is a principle of power in all intelligent beings, according to the Prophet Joseph Smith (see *Lectures on Faith* 1:13). Faith is also defined as a belief or knowledge coupled with action. As you exercise faith in Christ through your righteousness, your faith will increase.

When we have true faith, God blesses us with miracles, ministering angels, spiritual gifts, and every conceivable good thing. You would be wise to remember that signs follow believers who have already placed their faith in the true God.

In chapter 11 of the book of Hebrews we read, "By faith Abel offered unto God a more excellent sacrifice than Cain, by which he obtained witness that he was righteous, God testifying of his gifts: and by it he being dead yet speaketh" (Hebrews 11:4).

Elsewhere in this chapter of scripture, we review that by faith "Enoch was translated that he should not see death." By faith Noah, being warned by God of things not seen yet, "prepared an ark to the saving of his house." By faith Sara "received strength to conceive seed, and was delivered of a child when she was past age." By faith "Abraham, when he was tried, offered up Isaac." By faith Moses chose "to suffer affliction with the people of God, [rather] than to enjoy the pleasures of sin for a season" in the palace of Pharaoh, where he had been reared. By faith he led his people through the Red Sea as if on dry land. By faith "the walls of Jericho fell down, after they were compassed about seven days."

Wise counsel is given in the Book of Mormon: "Dispute not because ye see not, for ye receive no witness until after the trial of your faith. . . . For if there be no faith among the children of men God can do no miracle among them; wherefore, he showed not himself until after their faith. . . . And neither at any time hath any wrought miracles until after their faith; wherefore they first believed in the Son of God." (Ether 12:6, 12, 18.)

To know Jesus Christ is to love him. To love him is to keep his commandments. Keeping his commandments proves his wisdom and builds our trust and faith in him. Living the gospel proves that Jesus keeps his promises to you as you keep the covenants you made at baptism.

In ancient America some of the greatest wisdom uttered to mankind was contained in the words of good King Benjamin to his people (see Mosiah 2–5). This was about 125 years before Christ appeared to the righteous Nephites following his crucifixion in Jerusalem. King Benjamin did all he could to prepare his people for the fulfillment of the prophecy regarding the coming of Jesus Christ to the earth. He taught the people to believe in Christ even though they might not see him. They were to obey Christ's commandments even though the word came to them not from Jesus himself but rather through his appointed servants. This required great faith, but King Benjamin was willing to guide the people to achieve this important and sacred state of belief.

The record says that the words King Benjamin used to teach the people were inspired. They had been "delivered unto him by the angel of the Lord" (Mosiah 4:1).

People then were reminded that they were to obtain for themselves a knowledge of—

- The reality of Jesus Christ.
- The goodness of God and his matchless power.
- The wisdom, patience, and inimitable love of God.
- God's long-suffering attitude and forbearance with mankind.
- Jesus Christ's atonement.
- The value in trusting Jesus Christ.

King Benjamin also urged that people be diligent in keeping the Lord's commandments and that they continue in faith in Jesus always and forever. Jesus knows each of us!

Joseph Millett, an early member of the restored Church, had powerful faith in the Lord and was committed to doing his will. He spent his life serving in the gospel cause. One incident that he recorded in his personal journal occurred in 1871 while the Millett family was colonizing Spring Valley, Nevada. He wrote:

> One of my children came in, said that Brother Newton Hall's folks were out of bread. Had none that day. I put . . . our flour in sack to send up to Brother Hall's. Just then Brother Hall came in. Says I, "Brother Hall, how are you out for flour." "Brother Millett, we have none." "Well, Brother Hall, there is some in that sack. I have divided and was going to send it to you. Your children told mine that you were out." Brother Hall began to cry. Said he had tried others. Could not get any. Went to the cedars and prayed to the Lord and the Lord told him to go to Joseph Millett. "Well, Brother Hall, you needn't bring this back if the Lord sent you for it. You don't owe me for it." *You can't tell how good it made me feel to know that the Lord knew that there was such a person as Joseph Millett.* (Quoted in Eugene England, *Why the Church Is As True As the Gospel* [Salt Lake City: Bookcraft, 1986], p. 30, emphasis added.)

If the eye of the Lord is on the sparrow, surely he knows each of his children by name (see Matthew 10:29–32). He has pleaded with us to learn of him and to have faith in him so that miracles can bless our lives. He has said, "Be still and know that I am God" (Doctrine and Covenants 101:16).

Can anyone or anything separate the true believer from the love of Christ? The Apostle Paul wondered if tribulation, distress, persecution, famine, nakedness, or any peril could separate us from Christ.

Then Paul answered his own question by stating: "For I am persuaded, that neither death, nor life, nor angels, nor principalities, nor powers, nor things present, nor things to come, nor height, nor depth, nor any other creature, shall be able to separate us from the love of God" (Romans 8:38–39; see also verses 35, 37).

To believe this is to come to a certain fulness of faith. Consider how understanding these four vital truths about Jesus Christ will increase your own faith:

1. Jesus created the earth. He also created all that is on it—all growing things and creatures of the earth, sky, and water. He created the balance of nature for the good of all living things.

2. Jesus came to earth as the infant born of Mary through the power of the Holy Ghost. He was the Father's Only Begotten in the flesh. Jesus grew, learned, waxed strong, and became wise. He taught others and blessed them with miracles. He was forgiving. He established his church with twelve Apostles—the prototype for the restored gospel and Church today. Jesus testified that God the Father was Heavenly Father to us all. He endured the mighty suffering that was requisite for his atoning sacrifice.

3. Jesus lives in heaven with God the Father now. He leads, reveals, and inspires his prophets and his people on earth today so that his work may be accomplished—bringing to pass the immortality and eternal life of mankind.

4. Jesus is our Mediator with Heavenly Father. In his name we pray to God. Many moving and spontaneous testimonies are shared by people who know the reality of Jesus Christ and declare that he is their Redeemer. They know this from experience, from scripture study, and through the power of the Holy Ghost.

If we believe in him, believe what he has said to us, and act according to that belief, we do not have to suffer eternally for our sins. He was crucified and resurrected so that we might all live again after this life.

In summary, the crowning counsel you can receive as practical help for daily life is what King Benjamin emphasized to his people in ancient America shortly before he died:

- Believe in God.
- Believe that he is.
- Believe that he created all things, both in heaven and in earth.

- Believe that he has all wisdom and all power, both in heaven and in earth.
- Believe that man does not comprehend all the things that the Lord can comprehend. (See Mosiah 4:9.)

Measure any question put forth by man or any trial under the heavens that may come into your life against this scripture and surely your faith in God will increase. Apply it and you see you will not be led astray. When you believe in God, when you have faith in the Lord Jesus Christ, he will rush to be gracious to you.

10

Christ's Call to Repent

Repentance is the second principle of the gospel of Jesus Christ. The very plan of salvation provided for mankind's experience on earth is a gospel of repentance: it's about becoming ever better and better!

There are at least three reasons why repentance is an important principle from God and a blessing for mankind.

1. This life is the time to prepare to meet God (see Alma 12:24). This life is the time for people to learn, to grow, and to recognize their accountability for choices. An accountable person cannot enter the kingdom of heaven without repenting from sin and error.

2. No unclean thing can enter the kingdom of heaven. The Spirit cannot abide evil; that is, it cannot function and empower an individual who has chosen to follow evil in character and disposition, in choices of entertainment, and in attaining selfish desires and thwarting the work of God. Such things are inimical to God's plan for mankind and have no part in the glorious kingdom we speak of as heaven. Furthermore, the Holy Ghost cannot dwell in an impure person.

3. Covenants made with God are broken through sin. Repentance is necessary to restore those promises and blessings to the sinner.

Why does this happen, this sinning or falling away?

Many people do not yet know the fulness of the gospel. They

69

don't understand the catastrophe consequent to following today's values and lifestyles. God exists whether anyone believes in him or not. His principles are of eternal value and remain commandments for the good of his children whether mankind accepts that fact or not.

People can't live up to what they don't know. Hence the mission of the Church is manifest in part through perfecting the Saints and proselyting so that others may be gathered into the cause of truth.

Some people through rebellion withdraw from the Lord's Spirit; the Holy Ghost can then no longer strive with them. Once a person has had the Spirit and deliberately makes choices inconsistent with the gospel of Jesus Christ without repenting, only misery lies ahead.

Some people through ignorance of God's way and his laws for true happiness, move along life's path in abject misery. Jesus described all these types of people in the parable of the sower:

> When any one heareth the word of the kingdom, and understandeth it not, then cometh the wicked one, and catcheth away that which was sown in his heart. This is he which received seed by the way side.
>
> But he that received the seed into stony places, the same is he that heareth the word, and . . . with joy received it;
>
> Yet hath he not root in himself, but dureth for a while: for when tribulation or persecution ariseth because of the word, by and by he is offended.
>
> He also that received seed among the thorns is he that heareth the word; and the care of this world, and the deceitfulness of riches, choke the word, and he becometh unfruitful.
>
> But he that received seed into the good ground is he that heareth the word, and understandeth it; which also beareth fruit. (Matthew 13:19–23; see also verses 1–18.)

I can imagine the Lord looking upon you, a new member of his Church, and saying, "Blessed are your eyes, for they see; and your ears, for they hear." He loves all of his people and continues to strive with us so we may understand; so we may feel the warmth of his Spirit; so we may be worthy of the Holy Ghost, who governs our conscience; so we may succeed now and hereafter. Like an anxious parent who prays his teenager home safely, the Lord yearns after us and provides help so we can make it through life until we are "safely dead."

Repentance is about "making it." Heavenly Father and Jesus love each of us and want us to succeed in the challenge of life on this earth. They love us not because we are great and good and perfect but rather because *they* are. The quality of loving we can enjoy is in direct proportion to how much we have become like the Savior.

Through study, faith, and obedience to God's principles, ordinances, and commandments, you will come to understand why purity and goodness are necessary in the Lord's work. Joy comes. Inspiration will be present in your life. Your service in Christ's name to others will be inspired and follow God's direct course for his children.

The word *repent* is from the Latin stem *pentir,* "to be sorry." However, in the gospel sense there is another level. It means turning away from and changing the behavior that brought you sorrow. The challenge is to learn God's standard of behavior, recognize your mistakes or admit a fault, and be motivated to move forward in changing.

If you walk too closely to the edge of the adversary's kingdom, you can be in real danger of falling victim to foolish or even dangerous enticements. Reaching for Satan instead of Christ is a sign that you may have already lost the Spirit and cannot accurately judge your own condition. This is a dangerous time because you can become even deeper enmeshed in sin and stupidity and ever more incapable of change.

It is tragic when someone loses that precious power to tell the difference between right and wrong. The prophet Mormon taught that the devil "is an enemy unto God, and fighteth against him continually, and inviteth and enticeth to sin, and to do that which is evil continually" (Moroni 7:12). When a person falls victim to such enticing, without repentance he finds discipleship of Christ increasingly difficult: "Wherefore, a man being evil cannot do that which is good; neither will he give a good gift. For behold, a bitter fountain cannot bring forth good water; neither can a good fountain bring forth bitter water; wherefore, a man being a servant of the devil cannot follow Christ; and if he follow Christ he cannot be a servant of the devil. . . . That which is evil cometh of the devil; for the devil is an enemy unto God." (Moroni 7:10–12.)

Jesus said, "Except ye repent, ye shall all . . . perish" (Luke 13:3). Now, that is a stunning statement!

We know that all of us will die ultimately, but because of the atonement of Christ everyone will be resurrected as he was. Everyone will face judgment one day at the bar of God! If we haven't repented, we perish in the sense of being denied life in the presence of God and all the joyful adventures of eternity with him.

It is clear by comparison—once we admit to the divinity of Jesus Christ and are inspired by his words and his ways, we recognize certain things about ourselves that need changing. We need to repent! This is not something to be avoided; it is something to seek one on one with a beloved Savior.

Faith in the Savior leads inevitably to repentance. Because of your faith, baptism has already set you on a wonderful journey sparkling with new information, treasures of truth and enlightenment, and covenants and endowments for glorious blessings.

Truth and the witness of truth are received more readily when your spirit is cleansed and ready to be influenced by the Holy Spirit. Actually, until we repent we are all unable to grasp God's principles. Truth is revealed to us line upon line. Upon one strength another is built. As a new member of God's church, "if you keep [his] commandments, . . . you shall receive grace for grace" (Doctrine and Covenants 93:20).

Heaven is about peace and happiness. There is little peace and happiness when people make life miserable for others. Now is the time to examine your personal attitudes closely. With Jesus as our Redeemer and Savior, his call to repent should trigger a compelling echo that can only be quieted by our proper response to turn away from sin and feel sorry.

This is not an essay to take the wicked world to task. I merely want to point out that repentance is forever a necessity in this world. Baptism occurs only once, but repentance is needful daily, given the temptations and agonies imposed by the world and the inevitable lag in overcoming the detrimental habits of human nature. Every stage of spiritual development is reached through repentance as we reconcile our behavior with revealed truth.

For example, I recall a sacred gathering where new leadership was being blessed and set apart by the First Presidency of the Church. Following this procedure, the leaders were invited to introduce their family members. One of the women said, "This is my husband So and So. This is my daughter So and So. This is my son So and So." President Kimball stopped her and said, "Sister, could you say 'our' son or 'our' daughter?"

The woman was humbled, apologetic, and agreed to the suggestion at once. "Of course, President Kimball. Certainly!" And she took up her introductions again in the same fashion as before *as if the prophet had not corrected her!* She meant well—as we all do about over-coming a mistake—but habit was stronger than intentions.

Our life's battle with sin and stupidity may be kindly listed as a game of missed opportunities. One of the saddest moods of mankind is brought on by considering what might have been.

I recall overhearing a ballet teacher commiserating with a young student about negligence in attending her ballet class. "Oh, yes," said the teacher, "I forgive you for missing so many classes, Mary Anne, but can you forgive yourself? After all, you will never get up on your toes now." The young girl's body had gone past the time of toe training.

A young athlete had dreamed all his life of playing quarterback for Ohio State. He had the physique, the coordination, and the sense of the game. However, he did not have the will or understanding to make right choices. By missing high school graduation, he disqualified himself from college entrance, let alone team positions in a top univer-sity's football squad.

A moment's forbidden pleasure closes the door for young mission-ary experience. The Lord forgives, but the time for preparation is past.

There is an old saying worth remembering in the context of repen-tance: "That which is good, you pay for before you get it; that which is bad, you pay for after you get it and it usually costs more than you ex-pect."

It is good to recall that sin isn't hurtful because it is forbidden; rather, it is forbidden because it is hurtful. Any thought, choice, or ac-tion that draws you away from God is hurtful.

There is a very real war under way between good and evil. It takes many forms among nations and individuals. Satan desires to destroy the effectiveness of Jesus Christ's redeeming mission. Satan is particularly in-terested in those who are converted, who know not only that Christ does live but also that he loves everyone. Such believers stoutly declare themselves his disciples, willing to help in this saving work among men. *These* Satan would bring down to ineffectiveness through sin.

God's rules and regulations—his commandments to us for our own good—apply to all. They are the basis for appropriate social in-teraction between man and man as well as man and God. God is our creator. His is the plan we live under. He has the answers. He points the way. He pleads but then waits for us to choose the way of right-eousness or the way of Satan and perishing!

On the title page of a British edition of C. S. Lewis's thought-provoking book on the battle between good and evil, *The Great Divorce,* appears the following statement by the great teacher and English literary figure George MacDonald: "No, there is no escape. There is no heaven with a little of hell in it—no plan to retain this or that of the devil in our hearts or our pockets. Out Satan must go, every hair and feather!"

We are not alone. Christ himself was tempted by Satan, but he is our example in his rejection of Satan's clever and wicked lures to disguised destruction. The Lord's plan of salvation for us provides the motivation to—

- Examine personal habits and thoughts.
- Consciously set any needed new goals.
- Study the gospel and listen to inspired leaders.
- Stand firm for truth.
- Move from the realm of temptation by changing friends, environment, or employment, if need be.
- Pray each night for forgiveness and each morning for strength to change, endure, and resist temptation.
- Give sincere gratitude for the principle of repentance.
- Repent!

You are responsible for your own sins, and for the recognition, repentance, and restitution of them. You are not punished for Adam's transgressions or anybody else's. You may be hurt by the mistakes of others, but God will hold you responsible only for your own unrepented errors. He said, "Have I any pleasure at all that the wicked should die? . . . and not that he should return from his ways, and live? . . . Cast away from you all your transgressions, . . . and make you a new heart and a new spirit: . . .wherefore turn yourselves, and live ye." (Ezekiel 18:23, 31–32.)

"Turn yourselves!" the Savior said.

We have been called to repent so that we may be worthy of his Holy Spirit to guide and protect us now and so that we will prove worthy to dwell with him in heaven after death. He promises his forgiveness. He offers us redemption and salvation through his miraculous atonement; thus, our pains for sinning can be eased by his carrying our burden. It remains for us simply to accept his sacrificial gift.

Repent—do not perish! Repent and feel his redeeming love.

11

Christ's Redeeming Love

A favorite hymn among Latter-day Saints expresses the feelings of a person who has sinned and suffered the dreadful pangs of remorse and then, through repentance, been flooded with the inimitable sweetness of Christ's redeeming love and forgiveness:

> I stand all amazed at the love Jesus offers me,
> Confused at the love that so fully he proffers me.
> I tremble to know that for me he was crucified,
> That for me, a sinner, he suffered, he bled and died.
>
> (Charles H. Gabriel, "I Stand All Amazed," *Hymns,* no. 193.)

Oh, to bask in his redeeming love is indeed a miracle!

Who hasn't sinned? Even small sins need to be erased. Yet comparatively few ever really pay the price of real repentance and receive the miracle of God's forgiveness.

Saying "I'm sorry" is not enough. True, it helps—it is socially correct and may pacify the offended. However, dealing with God is far deeper than a swipe across a dirty face to take off surface soil. This requires a full change of heart. A truly repentant person must feel sufficient remorse for healing and purification, which strengthen determination to avoid repeating the sin.

We understand that God loves the sinner but not the sin. What I'm emphasizing here is that unless the sinner rejects the sin, asks forgiveness, and changes his ways, that person is doomed for ruin and misery, sooner or later.

It is an irrevocable law.

The gospel can help us to overcome sins of both omission and commission. Repentance includes not repeating the sins and determining absolutely to keep God's commandments. Once the slate is clean and the relief of God's love and forgiveness has been felt, the person is free to once again grow spiritually.

Many have said that after they were excommunicated from the Church because of breaking commandments, they truly felt the buffeting of Satan and sensed the lack of constant help from the Holy Ghost. This can be a most terrible time—emotionally, physically, and certainly spiritually. Terrible anguish can come when the Spirit withdraws because of sin, when there is a wedge between one's soul and heaven. The repentant person makes it a high priority to find confidence before God again, to quiet the rivers of torment coursing the mind, heart, and body.

A sensitive Christian person who has a very active conscience may, following a time of wrongdoing, finally endure a suffering as intense as Alma's exquisite and bitter pain as he suffered "for three days and for three nights . . . with the pains of a damned soul" (Alma 36:16). Relief finally came for Alma. After receiving the flood of forgiveness from God, Alma wrote, "On the other hand, there can be nothing so exquisite and sweet as was my joy"! (Alma 5:21.)

Enos sought divine remission of his sins and found strength to change his ways by turning to God. He had gone hunting in the forests of his homeland in ancient America. He was alone and had time to think about the things he had been taught by his father, including the admonitions of the Lord and the requisites for eternal life. Suddenly Enos felt a vivid hungering in his soul. He wrote, "I kneeled down before my Maker, and I cried unto him in mighty prayer and supplication for mine own soul; and all the day long did I cry unto him; yea, and when the night came I did still raise my voice high that it reached the heavens. And there came a voice unto me, saying: Enos, thy sins are forgiven thee, and thou shalt be blessed. And I, Enos, knew that God could not lie; wherefore, my guilt was swept away." When Enos asked the Lord how such a thing could be done, he was told that it was because of his faith in Christ, whom he had never seen. The Lord said, "Go to, thy faith hath made thee whole." (Enos 1:1–8.)

Consider the examples in the Bible when Jesus, noting the faith of those whom he had been teaching and healing, was filled with compassion. To one stricken with palsy he said, "Thy sins are forgiven thee." Then Jesus explained that he had the power on earth to forgive sins as well as to heal. Then, to emphasize the source of that power to the unbelieving scribes and Pharisees, he asked them whether it was as easy to say "Thy sins be forgiven" as to say "Rise up and walk." (Luke 5:18–26.)

After repentance before God, by his grace peace comes. Amulek offered a beautiful prayer for the Zoramites that we echo here: "May [you] begin to exercise your faith unto repentance, that ye begin to call upon his holy name, that he would have mercy upon you" (Alma 34:17).

There is another evidence of God's redeeming love. The repentant sinner can know that God remembers his sin no more! Consider these modern-day pronouncements: "I, the Lord, forgive sins, and am merciful unto those who confess their sins with humble hearts" (Doctrine and Covenants 61:2). "Behold, he who has repented of his sins, the same is forgiven, and I, the Lord, remember them no more" (Doctrine and Covenants 58:42).

Forgiveness is a gift through God's grace. Even though we must have a mind-set to submit and receive this magnificent gift, it is because he loves us that we receive this gift. Lowell L. Bennion has taught that a true Christian recognizes and accepts Christ's atonement. He said: "I like the literal meaning of the word 'atonement,' namely 'at/one/ment.' Man's goal is to become one with the Father and the Son, to bring his life in agreement with that of Deity. . . . To become one with the Father and the Son, we must overcome three things: mortality, sin, and ignorance, because the Father and Son are immortal, sinless, and intelligent." (*The Best of Lowell L. Bennion: Selected Writings 1928–1988,* ed. Eugene England [Salt Lake City: Deseret Book Co., 1988], p. 270.)

In his wonderful book entitled *The Miracle of Forgiveness,* President Spencer W. Kimball included a story of a man who had reached the stage of spiritual growth in his life where he wanted to right every one of his own wrongs. He wanted to get ready to meet his

Maker. However, when he was a young boy, his father had been an innocent victim of murder. As a boy and then through the long years of his life as a father himself, this man had hated the killer. He had been unable to forgive him as God required. Instead, he had tirelessly rehearsed the sufferings and shortcomings of his own entire life because his father had been murdered.

At last, mature in the gospel and seeking peace through forgiveness for his own sins, he went to the state prison to speak to the man who had forever changed his life by killing his father. His heart was warmed by the redeeming love of the Spirit within him. He was able to greet the prisoner with a calm patience that he had never felt before in this regard.

The two men talked for about an hour and a half as they reviewed that life-changing day thirty years before. Finally, the visitor confessed the personal resentment that he had suffered all these long years. He then humbly expressed his heartfelt change of attitude by saying that he forgave the murderer of his offense! Although this man was unsure of how the prisoner felt about his act of forgiveness, he himself was overcome with relief, and he wept at the fresh feeling of wholesomeness that came over him now that his heavy burden of bitterness and hatred was gone. Oh, how he was relieved at forgiving those who had sinned against him, as God required!

This man had gone through the steps of making his life right and had been marvelously rewarded with an inimitable feeling from God. (See *The Miracle of Forgiveness* [Salt Lake City: Bookcraft, 1969], pp. 289–93.)

President David O. McKay, concerned with the conditions on earth among men, quoted the English writer Beverly Nichols, who said, "Human nature *must* be changed on an enormous scale in the future. . . . And only Christ can change it." (*Stepping Stones to an Abundant Life,* comp. Llewelyn R. McKay [Salt Lake City: Deseret Book Co., 1971], p. 23.)

Missionary work involves far more than adding new members to the Church. It is about helping people become converted to Christ and to his glorious, joy-bringing principles. These principles, when followed, ensure the Lord's precious love, approval, and help in all aspects of our lives.

The following story illustrates the power of God to help people change:

Our family was contacted by the missionaries in Canada, and although Mom, my sister, and I soon accepted the gospel, it wasn't until after many months of discussions with the missionaries, reading the Book of Mormon that Dad received a testimony of the truthfulness of the gospel of Jesus Christ.

When the missionaries challenged us to be baptized just before Christmas, Dad hesitated. With all the celebrating he usually had done at this season, he wanted to wait until after the holidays. Alcohol and tobacco had been a normal part of his life, and he wanted to be certain that he could refuse them if faced with the enticement.

Dad did not have a problem with alcohol during the holidays, but he'd had his tobacco habit since he was twenty-four years old, and everything he'd ever tried to do to stop smoking only ended in disappointment, and this time was no exception.

When Dad saw how anxious we all were for baptism he agreed and did not tell the missionaries that he had not yet conquered tobacco. In fact, he didn't even tell us. We just assumed that he had quit.

Finally we arrived at the chapel on the day of the scheduled baptism. Dad was really jittery. He told us later that he wanted to be baptized but he also wanted a cigarette. He didn't know what to do. We went to change into our white clothing, but he lingered in the changing room and offered a prayer that the Lord would remove the craving for tobacco, because unless he did, Dad knew he would smoke again as soon as he was alone. Dad prayed constantly for the same blessing all during the baptismal service. Dad was the last one to be baptized. He told me later that when he came up out of the water he was still wanting a cigarette.

We changed back into dry clothing, and again, Dad lingered behind. This time he dropped to his knees and poured out his heart in prayer. He pled for Heavenly Father to erase his desire for smoking because he knew how many times he'd tried to quit on his own over many, many years.

Dad was the last member of the family to be confirmed a member of the Church. As the priesthood leaders lifted their hands from his head, Dad realized that the terrible craving to smoke was gone! As we walked outside from the church we passed someone who was smoking and Dad remarked that he was surprised that the smell of the smoke was offensive to him. (From a talk by Allen Marcov delivered 18 May 1991 on VISN; used by permission of the author.)

There are many who can testify of the healing, redeeming, and enabling love of the Savior that helped them to change from spirit-weakening ways. The Lord works from the inside out to help human nature change. When we take him into our lives, our spirit is changed by his redeeming love. Our behavior then follows suit.

In the fifth chapter of Alma in the Book of Mormon, the prophet Alma explains to his people the Lord's role in the conversion of their forefathers: "Behold, he changed their hearts; yea, he awakened them out of a deep sleep, and they awoke unto God. Behold, they were in the midst of darkness; nevertheless, their souls were illuminated by the light of the everlasting word; . . . and their souls did expand, and they did sing redeeming love" (Alma 5:7, 9).

Alma asked certain definitive questions of his people for their own preparation to meet God. I have adapted his questions to help you in your own self-examination (see Alma 5:6–33):

- Have you experienced a mighty change in your heart toward the Lord Jesus Christ and God the Father?
- Do you actually exercise faith in Christ?
- Have you felt the need to draw close to the Savior to repent from your weaknesses and sins?
- Do you believe in a life hereafter, when your mortal body will be raised in immortality to stand before God and be judged?
- Are you pure in heart, having repented of past sins?
- Are you learning to bridle all your passions that you may be filled with love?
- Do you perform righteous works and deal with your fellowman fairly?
- Are you free from persecution of others by force, gossip, or limiting their agency or opportunity?
- Have you been sufficiently humble, patient, and trusting in God's will?
- Have you been touched by the Holy Spirit? Have you felt to sing the song of redeeming love? Do you feel so now?

When Jesus traveled his homeland (a land we call *holy* today because it is where *he* walked, taught, and performed miracles), people flocked like sheep to their shepherd. They were drawn inexplicably to this master teacher and kindly friend. Not all who came were true believers or even seekers after truth—yet they came! Some came out of curiosity because they didn't understand. Others were restless with the uncomfortable forces at work in their lives. Some, perhaps, even plotted to discredit such a popular speaker of the day. Some came because they dared to call even the scribes and Pharisees to repentance! The lesson was taught that Jesus was no respecter of persons and that the Father loved all of his children.

Jesus also preached the amazing doctrine that there is great rejoicing in heaven among the angels over one sinner who repents!

The Savior emphasized this new doctrine (worth our recalling today) as he told the precious parables of the lost sheep, the lost coin, and the prodigal son with the father, who, when he saw the son returning and while "he was yet a great way off, . . . ran, and fell on his neck, and kissed him." This was in spite of all the son's wasteful, sinful, hurtful behavior. These parables remind us that even the least among us is of deep concern to the Lord of earth and heaven. (See Luke 15:1–32.)

Think about it—what thoughtful person doesn't hunt for a valuable possession whether it be of flock, field, wallet, or family? It is, as has been frequently noted, Christ's mission to redeem us all from the terrible though strengthening trials of this purposeful life. Whatever he teaches is for our good—if only we'll always listen and always hear and always do!

We know this analogy of the prodigal son to be important regarding our own great joy. Whenever we turn toward God in repentance, incredibly he rushes forth to welcome us. It is awesome. Wonderful. True! Such is his redeeming love.

And all heaven echoes this love when one of us repents.

12

True Baptism

Baptism is the third principle of the gospel (see Articles of Faith 1:4). When you are baptized in The Church of Jesus Christ of Latter-day Saints, you do more than offer a sign of accepting Christ. You make a covenant with Jesus to take upon you his name and his works and to keep his commandments so that you may always have his spirit with you. You promise to always remember him. Since baptism is such an important choice, you should learn all you can about true baptism as it is found in the Church today.

An interesting scripture speaks of people like you in another time. The prophet Alma had a goodly number of candidates for baptism in the Waters of Mormon. He gave a talk at these services to explain to the people what they were about to undertake (see Mosiah 18:7–17). It is the classic statement, really, about baptism. Let me emphasize certain phrases from that talk for you:

> Behold, here are the waters of Mormon . . . and now, as ye are desirous to *come into the fold of God,*
>   *and to be called his people;*
>   and are willing to *bear one another's burdens,* that they may be light;
>   yea, and are willing to *mourn with those that mourn;*

yea, and *comfort those that stand in need of comfort,*
and to *stand as witnesses of God* at all times and in all things,
and in all places . . . ,
that ye may be redeemed of God,
and be numbered with those of the first resurrection,
that ye may have eternal life, . . .
being baptized . . . as a witness before him that ye have entered into a covenant with him.
that *ye will serve* him
and *keep his commandments,*
that he may pour out his Spirit more abundantly upon you.
(Mosiah 18:8–10.)

Some years later in the land Bountiful, another scene relevant to baptism takes place. It is a highly dramatic scene. Pageants have tried to do it justice. The pure imaginings of the heart and mind may be even better for you.

The land Bountiful in ancient America was a desirable land that ran from the east to the west sea. The city had wealthy trade, sophistication, comforts, and industry of many kinds. But the people had become so caught up in their own success and cleverness that they scoffed at, and in some cases destroyed, many prophets and teachers who warned them that if they did not change their ways they would be destroyed along with their cities and fine things. Does that sound familiar? How often such a warning has come and how often people have refused to listen. Rome. Jerusalem. Babylon. Sodom and Gomorrah. Is America listening today?

At any rate, the land Bountiful in ancient America was destroyed in about A.D. 34, along with its great cities such as Zarahemla, Moroni, Gilgal, Onihan, Gadiandi, Jacob, and the city of Bountiful. This was because of the people's wickedness and abominations. This massive destruction happened in America while Christ was being crucified in Jerusalem. Destruction was felt across the world, and the land and its shape were changed forever. When the quaking of the earth ceased and the roar of the wild storm subsided; when the crash of falling trees quieted; when disrupted monuments, towers, and bridges settled, there was an ominous silence for many hours. The survivors—who were not buried up in the earth, drowned in the depths of the sea, burned by fire, fallen upon and crushed to death, carried away in a whirlwind, or overpowered by vicious poisonous vapors in the dreaded darkness—were the more righteous Nephites.

Many of these survivors gathered together about the temple in the land Bountiful. They marveled at the great changes that had occurred. They conversed about this Jesus Christ of whose death this destruction was a prophesied sign.

As they stood thus, a voice from heaven filled the air. The people heard it but did not understand at first what was being said. Even though it was a small voice it pierced their very beings. Three times the voice came to them. The third time, the people, now very attentive, *did* understand. It was the voice of God the Father introducing his Son! "Behold my Beloved Son, in whom I am well pleased, in whom I have glorified my name—hear ye him" (3 Nephi 11:7). As he spoke, the people "saw a Man descending out of heaven" (3 Nephi 11:8). He wore a white robe, and he stretched forth his hand toward them as he spoke: "Behold, I am Jesus Christ whom the prophets testified shall come into the world" (3 Nephi 11:10). Then Jesus invited the people to come forth and thrust their hands into his side and feel the sword wounds. They were invited also to feel the prints of the crucifixion nails in his hands and feet. He wanted them to know, he said, that he was the God of Israel and of the whole earth, who had been slain for the sins of the world. The people were overcome through the spirit and the tenderness of such an experience. When all had touched him, they were ready to listen as he began to teach.

Jesus taught the Nephites repentance and baptism; some form of the word *baptize* is used at least ten times in 3 Nephi 11. That is the importance that Jesus himself gave to this principle. He also gave the authority to Nephi and to some others that they might act as his agents in baptizing all who were converted to the Savior and who would repent.

In the Holy Land Jesus was baptized even though he was without sin. He was baptized to do the will of Heavenly Father, to "fulfill all righteousness" (Matthew 3:15), to be an example to us. When we are at least eight years of age, we too can be baptized out of obedience to that essential example.

Following his resurrection, Jesus continued to emphasize baptism. He appeared to his Apostles and commanded them to go into all parts of the world and unto all nations to teach the people and to baptize them "in the name of the Father, and of the Son, and of the Holy Ghost" (see Matthew 28:16–20; Mark 16:14–16).

Baptism has always been an essential ordinance for Heavenly Father's children. Adam was commanded to be baptized in the name of Jesus Christ. Adam asked the Lord, "Why is it that men must repent and be baptized in water?" And God said, "Therefore I give unto you a commandment, to teach these things freely unto your children, saying: That by reason of transgression cometh the fall, which fall bringeth death, and inasmuch as ye were born into world by water, and blood, and the spirit, which I have made, and so became of dust a living soul, even so ye must be born again into the kingdom of heaven, of water, and of the Spirit, and be cleansed by blood, even the blood of mine Only Begotten; that ye might be sanctified from all sin, and enjoy the words of eternal life in this world, and eternal life in the world to come, even immortal glory. For by the water ye keep the commandment; by the Spirit ye are justified, and by the blood ye are sanctified, therefore it is given to abide in you." (Moses 6:53, 58–61.)

Enoch had a vision in which he conversed with the Lord regarding his duties as a prophet. In his own record Enoch wrote: "And the Lord said unto me: Go to this people, and say unto them—Repent, lest I come out and smite them with a curse, and they die. And he gave unto me a commandment that I should baptize in the name of the Father, and of the Son, which is full of grace and truth, and of the Holy Ghost, which beareth record of the Father and the Son." (Moses 7:10–11.)

Baptism is a sacred ordinance that is not optional. The English word *baptize* comes from a Greek word that means to immerse or dip. The ordinance of baptism by immersion was restored in our time during the translating of the Book of Mormon from the gold plates. Baptism was mentioned on those plates. Joseph had a strong desire for greater knowledge on the subject. One day in May of 1829, Joseph and his scribe, Oliver Cowdery, went into the woods to pray about the matter of baptism.

Joseph later recorded that while the two were earnestly praying for understanding of this sacred subject, a "being" who identified himself as John the Baptist appeared to them and talked to them. He laid his hands upon their heads and conferred upon them "the Priesthood of Aaron, which holds the keys of the ministering of angels, and of the gospel of repentance, and of baptism by immersion for the remission of sins" (Doctrine and Covenants 13:1). The two men then baptized each other and later baptized others, including the Prophet's brother

Hyrum. From then on the ranks of The Church of Jesus Christ of Latter-day Saints have swelled through baptism. Only pure, innocent little children who have not yet reached the age of accountability do not need to be baptized (see Moroni 8:5–26). Everyone else does!

So vital is the Lord's baptism for everyone that proxy baptism for the dead was revealed to Joseph Smith. Provision was subsequently made for vicarious baptism to be done in the temple for those who died without a knowledge of the fulness of the gospel. Records of this work are carefully kept on earth and are binding in heaven. This is one way that turns the hearts of the children to their fathers or ancestors, and it is a link that strengthens the family line.

Today baptism for the dead is done in the temples in fonts dedicated for this purpose. Each font is supported on the backs of twelve oxen. These oxen represent the twelve tribes of Israel and are a reminder of the covenant the Lord made with his people regarding the great gathering of the tribes in the latter days and a restoration of the status of the children of Israel.

A sacred event of baptism for the dead took place many years ago in the St. George Temple, the first temple dedicated after the pioneers came. A painting by Harold I. Hopkins hangs in the foyer of this temple and is a moving record of this historic happening.

In 1877, Elder Wilford Woodruff, who later became President of the Church, was president of the St. George Temple. In August of that year, the spirits of many of America's Founding Fathers gathered around him while he was in the temple. President Woodruff later recalled: "Every one of those men that signed the Declaration of Independence, with General Washington, called upon me . . . two consecutive nights, and demanded at my hands that I should go forth and attend to the ordinances of the House of God for them" (in Conference Report, April 1898, pp. 89–90).

On 21 August 1877, Elder Woodruff and his assistant, J.D.T. McAllister, performed the proxy baptisms and confirmations for those great men, along with other prominent men in history, including many of the presidents of the United States. Also, Lucy Bigelow Young was baptized for seventy eminent women in history, including Martha Washington.

Baptismal fonts in modern temples are similar to those of ancient times. For example, in the ancient temple of Solomon, a deep basin "stood upon twelve oxen . . . and all their hinder parts were inward" (1 Kings 7:25).

Baptism for the dead was somewhat widespread in early Christianity. A reference that has baffled scholars for generations is found in a letter that Paul wrote to the Corinthians. He was trying to settle a question for those who did not believe in the resurrection. "Else what shall they do which are baptized for the dead, if the dead rise not at all? why are they then baptized for the dead?" (1 Corinthians 15:29.) The meaning of baptism for the dead was lost for all those generations until it was restored to The Church of Jesus Christ of Latter-day Saints from God through the Prophet Joseph Smith.

Baptism is a lifeline to heaven in that it opens the door for every other ordinance that God has given us and is necessary for exaltation in the life after this. Baptism has been a commandment of God for his children since earliest times.

Baptism that is acceptable before the Lord has never changed. Though you may have been baptized, even by immersion, into another religious denomination, that baptism is not valid in The Church of Jesus Christ of Latter-day Saints. Proper language and procedure, as decreed by the Lord, and true authority from God to perform the ordinance are necessary for it to be acceptable to the Lord. These are found only in The Church of Jesus Christ of Latter-day Saints.

The *Encyclopedia of Mormonism* includes the following information about the baptismal covenant:

> When a person enters into a Latter-day Saint baptism, he or she makes a covenant with God. Baptism is a "sign . . . that we will do the will of God, and there is no other way beneath the heavens whereby God hath ordained for man to come to Him to be saved" (*Teachings of the Prophet Joseph Smith,* p. 198).
>
> Candidates promise to "come unto the fold of God, and to be called his people, . . . to bear one another's burdens, . . . to mourn with those that mourn, and . . . to stand as witnesses of God . . . even until death" (Mosiah 18:8–9). A person must enter this covenant with the proper attitudes of humility, repentance, and determination to keep the Lord's commandments, and serve God to the end (2 Nephi 31:6–17; Moroni 6:2–4; Doctrine and Covenants 20:37). In turn, God promises remission of sins, redemption, and cleansing by the Holy Ghost (Acts 22:16; 3 Nephi 30:2). This covenant is made in the name of the Father, the Son, and the Holy Ghost.
>
> The baptized can renew this covenant at each sacrament

meeting by partaking of the sacrament. This continual willingness to remember Christ and to keep his commandments brings the Lord's promise of his Spirit and produces the "fruits" (Galatians 5: 22) and "gifts" (Doctrine and Covenants 46) that lead to eternal life. ("Baptismal Covenant" by Jerry A. Wilson. Reprinted with permission of Macmillan Publishing Company from *Encyclopedia of Mormonism,* edited by Daniel H. Ludlow, vol. 1, pp. 94–95. Copyright © 1992 by Macmillan Publishing Company.)

Baptism is ordained of God for the blessing of man.
By way of summary, let me review the following points:

• Being baptized and confirmed are public acts of your private promises or covenants with the Lord. Your choices and behavior are now consequential and answerable by you before God.
• Being baptized and confirmed are marks of personal progress. You are given a fresh start to live purely according to the true principles of the gospel of Jesus Christ.
• Being baptized and confirmed will strengthen you to live after the manner of a disciple of Christ, to take his name upon you and always remember him, and keep the commandments which he has given you.
• You will feel peace and a life-changing power through a closer relationship with the Lord.
• Your compassion will increase for others who struggle for their lives without valid answers to life's problems. As you learn more, you can share more.
• Your soul or your inner, eternal self will feel full of light, and you will hunger and thirst after knowledge of the kingdom of God.
• You will find yourself seeking the additional ordinances, principles, and blessings available to members of the Church.
• You will find a wholesome support system in the Church among friends and associates.
• You will be welcome, indeed, and grow increasingly comfortable with this remarkable life.

A careful and consistent review of these things brings renewal of spirit and remembrance of the privilege that it is to be baptized a member of The Church of Jesus Christ of Latter-day Saints. The covenants made with the Savior are sacred and life-changing.

13

Confirmation and the Gift of the Holy Ghost

The fourth principle of the gospel is the laying on of hands for the gift of the Holy Ghost, which takes place at confirmation.

Confirmation completes the process of baptism. Remember, Jesus taught that a person must be baptized by the water and the Spirit (see John 3:5), which is to say that a candidate for baptism is immersed under the water, totally and every whit, and then the confirmation takes place soon thereafter. One is not without the other.

Confirm means "to make more sure."

Confirmed. Ratified. Established. Secured. Substantiated. Verified. And welcomed as a member of The Church of Jesus Christ of Latter-day Saints! This is what it means to be confirmed—it is at once a reminder of status and a rite of passage.

During confirmation the head is bowed, and eyes are closed in reverence. In this moment of prayer and blessing, the new convert is ready to feel and learn and receive.

Here are some questions and answers as a guide to help you understand and value confirmation and the gift of the Holy Ghost.

Q. When does confirmation occur?

A. Soon after baptism. It may happen as soon as you are changed from your baptismal clothing. It may happen at the next fast and testimony meeting in your ward. This is worked out with the priesthood leader according to your desires.

Q. How is this done?

A. Men holding the Melchizedek Priesthood will stand in a circle about you and place their hands upon your head as you sit on a chair. You should close your eyes in reverence, because God is addressed in the prayer.

Q. What do these men say?

A. One of the men will call you by your full name and tell you that in the name of Jesus Christ and with the authority of the Melchizedek Priesthood that they hold, they confirm you a member of The Church of Jesus Christ of Latter-day Saints. In the same manner, by "the laying on of hands," they bestow the gift of the Holy Ghost. It is a most sacred time of your life.

Q. What words are actually used to give me the gift of the Holy Ghost?

A. "Receive the Holy Ghost!"

Q. What is the Holy Ghost?

A. The Holy Ghost is the third member of the Godhead, but unlike Heavenly Father and Jesus Christ, the Holy Ghost is a personage of spirit and not flesh and bones. Though you cannot see him, you can certainly feel his influence. (Doctrine and Covenants 130:22.)

Q. What does that really mean? How do I receive the Holy Ghost?

A. It means that in your heart you are to humbly and consciously accept this sacred, remarkable gift given to you by God through his servants. Likely you will feel a sense of peace, warmth, a new spiritual strength, or perhaps a fluttering of your heart, but as you learn to *use* the gift of the Holy Ghost to benefit yourself and mankind—as it falls within your sphere to do so—you will come to understand better the nature of the gift of the Holy Ghost.

Q. How does it feel to have the Holy Ghost?

A. It is a different feeling at different times and perhaps different in different people. You may hear a still whisper or a firm command. You may feel a kind of burning in your heart. You may have sudden inspiration or a quickening of understanding. Such understanding may come to your mind as you are reading scripture or teaching a lesson. You may feel as if a warm cloak is securely wrapped about you. You may weep. You may have a quiet, calm, peaceful feeling. This is a very personal thing and should be considered a sacred experience. Care should be used in talking about such an occurrence—only when moved upon by the Spirit. The influence of the Holy Ghost, in whatever way it comes to you, is remarkable and wonderful. Once you have recognized that influence, you will surely miss it if it leaves. As has been said, that happens if you do something wrong or if you just aren't concerned about his invaluable gift.

Q. When do I use the gift of the Holy Ghost?

A. As a member of the Church, there will be many opportunities to do so in your personal life and in helping others given to your care. Consider this: have you ever given someone a gift that they put aside, maybe even left it where it could be forgotten or even spoiled? This is how the Lord must feel when we neglect this marvelous gift. The more you use the gift of the Holy Ghost, the better it will be for you, the more you will value the gift and want to give thanks for it.

Q. Who has this gift?

A. Each person born to this world has the Light of Christ, whether it is effective in him or not, according to his life choice and understanding. The Light of Christ helps you to know right from wrong. The gift of the Holy Ghost is something more. Only those people who have been baptized and confirmed members of The Church of Jesus Christ of Latter-day Saints are given the gift of the Holy Ghost and can enjoy the variety of spiritual gifts accompanying it.

Q. What about this "variety of spiritual gifts"?

A. The Lord has said in relation to spiritual gifts: "Seek ye earnestly the best gifts, always remembering for what they are given; for verily I say unto you, they are given for the benefit of those who love me and keep all my commandments, and him that seeketh so to do; that all may be benefited that seek or that ask of me, that ask and not for a sign that they may consume it upon their lusts" (Doctrine and Covenants 46:8–9). Baptized and confirmed members who follow the Lord's counsel may enjoy such blessings as the gift of enlightenment, of witnessing that Christ lives and is the Redeemer, of healing, of tongues, of ministering angels, of warning, of discernment, of judgment between good and evil, of knowledge of spiritual truths! These are some of the spiritual gifts that come through the companionship of the Holy Ghost. Refer to Doctrine and Covenants 46 and 1 Corinthians 12:4–11 for additional perspective.

Q. Practically speaking, how can I keep the influence of the Holy Ghost?

A. To enjoy the constant influence of the Holy Ghost requires obedience and repentance. Being obedient makes you less vulnerable to

Satan's temptations. Repentance keeps you pure and confident before God. The Holy Ghost cannot function in an atmosphere of sin. The scriptures emphasize that "a man may receive the Holy Ghost, and it may descend upon him and not tarry with him" (Doctrine and Covenants 130:23). The reason it does not "tarry" is that wrong choices drive out the Holy Spirit.

Q. Why do we need the Holy Ghost?

A. We need the Holy Ghost to help us through the challenges of life and to guide us in our important spiritual development. The Lord speaks in our minds and hearts by the Holy Ghost. The gift of the Holy Ghost testifies of God, warns of danger and gives knowledge.

Life is a kind of school. We are here to learn and to increase in understanding of God's purposes for us. We grow when we have to make choices, reason things through, try again and again, endure all manner of disappointment, and survive temptation, pressure, and relationship demands. But we can cope better with life through this great gift of the Holy Ghost! Think of a baby as it learns to walk. The faltering steps, falling down, and getting up to try again is a process of muscle strengthening that assists the final outcome of upright mobility. As you pray for the Holy Ghost to be with you and as you heed its help, you will feel it with you again and again.

Q. How does the Holy Ghost help me?

A. As an example, pretend that you are visiting a World Expo in a strange city. You aren't certain where to go or what to see. You don't really know what is the best use of your time, energy, and resources. Then you take advantage of a special offer and rent a cassette that guides you and explains what you are seeing as you go along. You understand the interesting and beautiful experience more fully when you don't "go it alone." A personalized tour that speaks to you through earphones makes a difference. You are led through a maze of buildings. You are guided through crowds of strangers. You are steered past tempting diversions. You are kept from getting lost. If you should decide not to listen to the tape, you could get way off track and miss some of the best parts of the Expo.

The Holy Ghost is a spiritual guide who will whisper warnings, confirm truths, and witness that the Lord is close by and loves you.

Q. Does the Holy Ghost have any other name?

A. Yes. Names used when referring to the Holy Ghost include Comforter, Revelator, Sanctifier, Testator, Holy Spirit of Promise, the Holy Spirit.

Getting baptized and confirmed and then cultivating the gift of the Holy Ghost will bring you more blessings than you might imagine. Right now you are only a beginner at understanding. Sometime you will think about all this again. It may be just before you drop off to sleep at night. It may be in the next fast and testimony meeting in your ward. Or it may be while you are writing a personal record of your baptism. Suddenly a good feeling will warm your heart. You will know that the Lord is near you. You will feel that Jesus and Heavenly Father love you and are pleased with you. You will feel comforted that these things are true. This is a unique characteristic of eternal gospel principles. They are underlined by a feeling of rightness, comfort, and peace.

Just think about this incredible gift from God to you. For important insight, read the wonderful account of Adam's baptism in the Pearl of Great Price (see Moses 6:50–68). It gives the Lord's perspective, beneficial to your own experience. Speaking of the effects of baptism and the gift of the Holy Ghost upon the new convert, it says: "It is given to abide in you; the record of heaven; the Comforter; the peaceable things of immortal glory; the truth of all things; that which quickeneth all things, which maketh alive all things; that which knoweth all things, and hath all power according to wisdom, mercy, truth, justice, and judgment" (Moses 6:61).

Of the Holy Ghost one gospel scholar has written, "It is the office of the Holy Ghost to lift burdens, . . . extend hope, and reveal whatever is needed to those having claim on his sacred companionship." (*Encyclopedia of Mormonism,* ed. Daniel H. Ludlow, 5 vols. [New York: Macmillan, 1992], 2:650).

Like baptism, the rite of bestowing the gift of the Holy Ghost has been part of God's plan since earliest times. The word *confirmation* is not mentioned in the New Testament, but there are incidents recorded when converts were baptized and the Apostles laid their hands upon heads so that the new members might receive the Holy Ghost.

During the Last Supper with his disciples in Jerusalem, Christ sensed their deep sadness as he told them that his time had come to leave. He promised to send them a special Comforter and provided that all who would be baptized could receive this Comforter.

The variety of spiritual gifts that come with the companionship of the Holy Ghost is unlike any other blessing you will have ever received in your life. As life thereafter unfolds, this will prove to be a marvelous and unique blessing.

SECTION THREE

What You Need to Know

14

The Light of Life

Gospel intelligence and understanding often become priorities to the new convert or to anyone seeking truth to live by in a world of confused ideas. The ultimate good—the best direction, solace, inspiration, and motivation—come from the Lord. He is the light by which all men may see truth. It is through him and by him that every aspect of human experience is recognized for what it really is.

I have heard that sleepwalkers even in their own familiar surroundings can only guess where the chairs are, what objects they are feeling when they touch their desk top. For them, things are recognizable only when seen in the light. The light of the Lord works in a similar way in your life: it adds an additional perspective. It is a penetrating light that reveals beneath-the-surface truth!

Our dear Lord and Savior is compelling and constant in his invitation to "come unto me." "Walk with me in the meekness of my ways," he gently beckons. "I will be a light unto them forever that hear my words." To all who accept such invitations comes the promised enlightenment and peace, not further stumbling in darkness. The benefits of responding to such invitations seem exceedingly clear: when we follow Christ there shall be no lonely, misguided walk through any experience, not even life itself. Frustration will be eased and temptations more effectively avoided. We shall have the light of life, which is the companionship of the Creator of life, if we choose to hook into that source and switch on the power.

This power source, this light from Christ, is totally reassuring as it supplies a feeling of confidence that permeates every fiber of your being and reveals truth and error for what they are. This is the blessing of turning to the Lord for light and direction.

And at last, in the end—whenever it comes—you will be safely, surely guided back to the presence of the Lord and Heavenly Father with fewer bruises of the soul than if you had simply stumbled about in darkness.

A remarkable personal experience of Lorenzo Snow reveals his personal testimony about this subject:

> Some two or three weeks after I was baptized, one day while engaged in my studies, I began to reflect upon the fact that I had not obtained a knowledge of the truth of the work—that I had not realized the fulfillment of that promise, "he that doeth my will shall know of the doctrine," and I began to feel very uneasy. I laid aside my books, left the house, and wandered around through the fields under the oppressive influence of a gloomy, disconsolate spirit, while an indescribable cloud of darkness seemed to envelop me. I had been accustomed, at the close of day, to retire for secret prayer, to a grove a short distance from my lodgings, but at this time I felt no inclination to do so. The spirit of prayer had departed and the heavens seemed like brass over my head. At length, realizing that the usual time had come for secret prayer, I concluded I would not forgo my evening service, and, as a matter of formality, knelt as I was in the habit of doing, and in my accustomed, retired place, but not feeling as I was wont to feel.
>
> I had no sooner opened my lips in an effort to pray, than I heard a sound, just above my head, like the rustling of silken robes, and immediately the spirit of God descended upon me, completely enveloping my whole person, filling me from the crown of my head to the soles of my feet, and O the joy and happiness I felt! No language can describe the almost instantaneous transition from a dense cloud of mental and spiritual darkness into a refulgence of light and knowledge, that God lives, that Jesus Christ is the Son of God, and of the restoration of the Holy Priesthood, and the fullness of the Gospel. (Quoted in Preston

Nibley, *The Presidents of the Church* [Salt Lake City: Deseret Book Co., 1971], pp. 139–40.)

Your Friend, your Savior, your Lord, your God! Imagine!

Studying God's revealed word and then experimenting upon it or trying it out to see if it works is important. But drawing close to the Lord, and through him to Heavenly Father, gives light to life and your whole being. Even if your faith is tentative at first, if you follow him, trying out his counsel and commandments in exactness, the proof will come.

John Taylor, third President of the Church, is an example of one who followed the Lord all his life, at last becoming a prophet of God in the latter days. John was reared in England. As a young man he was driven by the idea that he had some special mission for which he had come to earth. He didn't know exactly how it would unfold, but he knew that nothing could really stop him from bringing people unto Christ—that is, nothing short of his own behavior.

He somehow knew that as long as he followed Christ he would be preserved and strengthened to accomplish his life's work. In 1831 young John Taylor booked passage for Canada. During the voyage, they encountered a week-long storm of such extreme severity that even the bravest souls were daunted. But John's confidence in his own destiny was so unwavering and his faith in the Lord so strong that he didn't fret about the possibility of the ship's sinking. As it turned out, both the ship and John weathered the storm.

This is a reminder to all who say they believe in Jesus Christ but "turn off the light" when it comes to a dark trial. They forget, they resist, they procrastinate, they are led carefully astray by the forces of evil or the consequences of their own poor choices. This is not true faith in an all-powerful God. This gospel is the only effective guide for someone who wants a relatively smooth life. We say "relatively" because life is about tribulations and personal growth. Only by demonstrating faith in the light of the gospel and its loving Author do we see those hard times for what they are so we can grow closer to God through them.

President David O. McKay testified that "no person can study this divine personality [Jesus], can accept his teachings without becoming conscious of an uplifting and refining influence within himself. In fact, every individual may experience the operation of the most potent force that can affect humanity." (*Cherished Experiences from the Writings of President David O. McKay,* comp. Clare Middlemiss [Salt Lake City: Deseret Book Co., 1976], p. 24.)

True Christians respond to the mellowing influence and also to the high discipline and selfless service that enhance one's own life! The result can be stable spirits, directed parents, and children with true values and goals growing up in households of love and faith. This is the bulwark against the disturbing foolishness, wickedness, and darkness of the world.

There is a remarkable precedent of the joy in drawing one's life under the light of the Lord. It is found in 4 Nephi in the Book of Mormon. This is the record of two hundred years or several generations when people lived according to the Light. There was a constant outpouring from the Holy Ghost, and they partook of the heavenly gifts so that marvelous miracles occurred. They did not argue or quarrel, and every man dealt justly one with another. They lived with each other in love, and "there were no envyings, nor strifes, nor tumults, nor whoredoms, nor lyings, nor murders, nor any manner of lasciviousness; and surely there could not be a happier people among all the people who had been created by the hand of God" (4 Nephi 1:16; see also verses 1–18).

Being in a congregation of Latter-day Saints can be about as close to that kind of happy people as is possible in the world today. But this group is a diverse group as well. All kinds of people are Mormons, and a congregation of Church members provides a mirror of life. The rain falls on the just and the unjust, so yes, there are problems typical of life. However, in such a congregation one also finds the John Taylors, those who can forgive and even forget, the stoics, the "loving anyway" folks, those who endure and stay at their posts no matter what. And there are serving, giving, compassionate people who help each other make it through each day.

Helena W. Larson was for many years the executive assistant to the general presidency of the Young Women organization of the Church. Shortly before her death in the fall of 1993, she prepared her personal testimony of the gospel and a record of her own experience with the blessing that comes when people help people in true personalized Christian service. She explains that during her high school years, illness had kept her from school and church and friends half of the time. She writes:

I couldn't participate and I didn't make friends or enter into their lives very well under these circumstances. I was a loner.

Only once did I try to break the pattern—by entering an MIA Speech contest. I was the only one who entered from our ward, so, without hearing my talk, the ward executives sent me to the stake contest, where I was a miserable failure. I decided then and there to stay within my shell, and not get hurt again.

But my Gleaner teacher decided differently. For the first time, I had a teacher who was not willing to let me sit silent in my corner. She was given the chairmanship of the program for the stake Gleaner banquet and immediately assigned me to the job of being toastmistress, deciding the theme, and suggesting topics for the responses. I told her I couldn't do it. "Yes you can," she assured me time after time, "because I'll help you every step of the way."

I loved her so much I was willing to try for her, although in my heart I knew I'd fail. First, she and I talked over possible themes. When we met with a committee of girls, however, she made me tell them my ideas. She claimed no part in them. I wrote out my continuity, and with her careful and loving suggestions, rewrote it many times until even I could see that it was good.

"But," I told her, "I can't stand up before three hundred girls and give this talk. I'll make a poor impression, and I'm not pretty or attractive, and I'll spoil your whole evening."

With an arm around me, she said, "That's utter nonsense; you'll be the star of the evening!"

So she heard me say my part many times, once even taking me to the Empire Room of the Hotel Utah to do it. She had arranged to have a microphone there so I could experience the actual setting. Then she asked to see the dress I would wear. She brought a corsage for me that night that not only matched the dress, but also lifted my spirits. She had her hairdresser do my hair in a way that would be more becoming to me.

But best of all, she knelt with me just before the event, and explained to the Lord that I was a lovely girl who had worked hard and that I needed His help to do a good job. How could I have failed with His and her love surrounding me?

And so Helen Spencer Williams, through love and personal work and sacrifice, started me on the road to normal associations with young people and to activity in the Church. When she went on the stake board, she recommended me as the teacher of her class. When she joined the general board, she recommended that I take her place on the stake board. And when she was put into the general presidency of the YWMIA, she recommended me for the general board!

President Thomas S. Monson said, "We learn that decisions determine destiny" ("Invitation to Exaltation," *Ensign,* June 1993, p. 4). Good decisions are based on God's principles. God's principles work because they are supplied by the Creator of man. He did not create us and send us forth to earth to wander aimlessly, unattended, and undirected!

He is the Light, the Answer! It remains for us to turn to this source. No one will be happy or saved in ignorance. Some trials come because people have not sought knowledge of the gospel. Sometimes adversity is imposed on a victim because of the undisciplined or uneducated action or decisions of others. Trouble and trials also may be God-allowed or heaven-helped according to his grander purposes, but if people live in his light, the outcome is always beneficial.

Gerald N. Lund is one of the great teachers of gospel doctrine. He also is a highly successful author. He said an important thing for each of us to remember: "No matter how clever, how sophisticated the philosophies of an anti-Christ may seem, they are not true. They are riddled with contradictions, errors, and false assumptions. . . . A believer need not apologize for his or her beliefs, for these beliefs withstand every scrutiny much more efficiently than do the doctrines of Satan." ("Countering Korihor's Philosophy," *Ensign,* July 1992, p. 21.)

Remember, there is truth in what we believe, teach, and do in the name of Jesus Christ. There is a continuum through all of human history that Jesus Christ the Redeemer is there for you—for you and your friends and loved ones. You are numbered and known to him yesterday, today, and always. It is for you to eagerly, speedily use your free agency to accept his light. If we seek gospel knowledge, try to emulate Christ in our lives, and obey his counsel, it will be midday bright always for us all along the journey.

15

The Articles of Faith

Many people of the world are stressed, depressed, and wandering aimlessly. Even the most educated and disciplined people often feel an emptiness and a lack of purpose in life. The responses of many visitors to the Church's various information centers, such as at Temple Square in Salt Lake City, Utah, confirm this. Many sense that Latter-day Saints have confidence about life, a sense of sure direction and peace before God that is almost awesome to those who have struggled through life philosophically.

Latter-day Saints have satisfying answers to difficult questions and solutions for personal problems.

They have a philosophy of hope and purpose in trying to endure—even with a certain grace—through trials.

They have incredible skills to share this point of view.

As a member of this Church, you may often find yourself in a position of respect, trust, and even envy. People will ask you what you have in your life that is so different from their own lives. This chapter is written to help you explain some of the Church's basic beliefs.

Some of what we believe is collected into a series of statements called the Articles of Faith. This collection has an interesting history.

The Church of Jesus Christ of Latter-day Saints was organized in 1830. It grew rapidly because people were ready for truth, and Joseph

Smith offered eternal truths simply and directly through the power of God. Within ten years missionaries had been sent to many nations of the world, including Palestine, the East Indies, England, Scotland, Wales, Europe, and Australia.

The success stirred an emigration movement to the United States by those who wanted to be near the center of truth. All of this caught the attention of the press and historians. Who were these people, and what did they believe? What was different about this new religion? Why did people follow Joseph Smith?

By 1839 a Mr. Bastow was planning to write a history of the State of New Hampshire. Many in the state had accepted the Book of Mormon and had joined the LDS church. To learn more about them, Mr. Bastow contacted his friend John Wentworth in Chicago. Mr. Wentworth was a newspaper editor but could not supply the information that Bastow wanted. But he had heard of Joseph Smith. Curious himself, John Wentworth wrote to the young Prophet for information.

The answer to this request became known as the Wentworth Letter. It is one of the most important documents in early Church literature.

Joseph told his own story and shared the beginnings of the Church and its subsequent growth. Then, in the last part of the letter, he spelled out some of the doctrines of the Church. This summary is now called the Articles of Faith. These thirteen statements of belief have since become canonized as scripture. They are published as part of the Pearl of Great Price, one of the four standard works of the Church. While they do not attempt to state every point of doctrine that we believe, they are clear, concise, forthright statements written under inspiration from God. They are a fine example of the spirit of revelation that rested upon Joseph Smith.

The Articles of Faith are memorized by each child who is preparing to turn twelve years old and move out of the Primary training program for children. They are studied and applied by adult members.

The following discussion of each article of faith should help you to strengthen your own growing testimony and to prepare you to better explain your beliefs to friends, family, and others.

1. We believe in God, the Eternal Father, and in His Son, Jesus Christ, and in the Holy Ghost.

Latter-day Saints are Christians.

A remarkable thing about the vision the fourteen-year-old boy

Joseph Smith had in answer to a sincere prayer was that he saw God the Father, and standing beside him was his Son, Jesus Christ. No longer need the world be confused about the nature of God!

Of course we are Christians! Knowing the nature and individuality of God the Father and God the Son, Jesus Christ, can bring great blessings.

Whether anybody believes in God, he is still there. He is our Father in Heaven. Jesus was the firstborn in the spirit and his only begotten in the flesh on earth! This Joseph learned on that first visit from those heavenly beings.

You, too, can know that God lives and that he loves you. He will answer your prayers. Through the power of the Holy Ghost you can have your own insight into the Godhead, your own witness that they are what Joseph himself saw in preparation for the restoration of the full gospel to earth for the benefit of all of God's children who would listen.

References to Study

> Bible: Matthew 3:16–17; Mark 9:7
> Book of Mormon: 3 Nephi 11:6–7, 25
> Doctrine and Covenants 130:22–23

2. We believe that men will be punished for their own sins, and not for Adam's transgression.

Or for Eve's, we might add! Adam and Eve were having a great time living effortlessly in a garden of peace, beauty, and plenty. Animals were tame, and feeling good was taken for granted. But Adam and Eve were likely not learning much in such a state. When they made their own choice to eat the fruit from the tree of knowledge—to know as the Gods knew—they also incurred the consequences of that choice: enemy animals, life by the sweat of the brow, mortal death. But oh! what a grand adventure is life!

The key idea for this article of faith is *agency*.

There are at least three points to understand concerning agency:

- The right to choose—or agency—is God's eternal gift to every person.
- Choice brings inevitable consequences. When we use our agency, we ought to want the consequences of the choice. We

will certainly get them, whether they bring joy or suffering, pleasure or pain, excitement or shame. You may choose, but you will pay for your mistakes or enjoy your wise choices.

• Choice often requires sacrifice in one form or another. There is no such thing as freedom from consequences.

References to Study

Bible: Galatians 6:7
Book of Mormon: 2 Nephi 2:27
Doctrine and Covenants 138:4
Pearl of Great Price: Abraham 3:24, 26

3. We believe that through the Atonement of Christ, all mankind may be saved, by obedience to the laws and ordinances of the Gospel.

The atonement of Christ has been widely considered, written about, and preached so that people may understand the incredible blessings that are ours because of Jesus' obedient and selfless sacrifice.

Jesus took upon himself, at Heavenly Father's command, the role of Savior and Redeemer of mankind. He suffered for our sins so that we would not have to suffer endless torment if we would repent and believe in Christ enough to follow after him. By example, Jesus taught us of the promise of resurrection. He had power over death, and yet he allowed himself to be crucified. Then he rose again on the third day, resurrected. Each of us will live again after we have died. How we live and what glory we will receive is up to us based upon what we know and what we choose to do (that is, how we use our agency). God's grace gives us opportunity, but our works will determine our status.

What a debt we owe Jesus! How deeply we should love and appreciate him!

References to Study

Bible: Isaiah 53:11; Acts 2:38
Book of Mormon: 2 Nephi 10:25; Mosiah 15:8

4. We believe that the first principles and ordinances of the Gospel are: first, Faith in the Lord Jesus Christ; second, Repentance; third, Baptism by immersion for the remission of sins; fourth, Laying on of hands for the gift of the Holy Ghost.

Because of the basic and profound effect the first principles and ordinances have on each individual, I have discussed them separately and at some length in chapters 4 through 9.

References to Study

> Bible: Hebrews 11; Mark 16:16
> Book of Mormon: 3 Nephi 11:23–26
> Doctrine and Covenants 130:23
> Pearl of Great Price: Moses 6:53–68

5. We believe that a man must be called of God, by prophecy, and by the laying on of hands by those who are in authority, to preach the Gospel and administer in the ordinances thereof.

For a church and the work of a church to be accepted by God, everything needs to be done in his way, according to his will, and by his power and authority.

To belong to a church with divine authority to bless, confirm, bestow, lead, and organize makes a great deal of difference. People mean well. Many churches are filled with conscientious members with devoted clergy. But there is a difference in the Church of Jesus Christ. We have authority and power from God.

In terms of our eternal life, whatever we do on earth should be acceptable in heaven. Leadership should be called by God's inspiration and his authority if they are to act in his name, and all ordinances and procedures should be done according to his will and ways.

References to Study

> Bible: Exodus 3:2–10
> Book of Mormon: Alma 31:36; Moroni 3:2–3
> Doctrine and Covenants 42:11

6. We believe in the same organization that existed in the Primitive Church, namely, apostles, prophets, pastors, teachers, evangelists, and so forth.

The Primitive Church refers to the Church established by Jesus when he was on the earth. This article of faith is a very important tenet. Look around at the world at God's children who are functioning in a state of confusion. You will see not just diversity; you will also see the contention that has erupted through the ages between religious movements. We hear of religious wars all about us from to-day's media.

Joseph Smith prayed in the grove to find out which church was true. There were so many conflicting views and arguments and forms of baptism and partial beliefs. Joseph was startled when he told his vision to his local clergy and they became incredibly angry. Religion had become a business, and God was not in them.

References to Study

> Bible: Ephesians 4:11
> Doctrine and Covenants 107

7. We believe in the gift of tongues, prophecy, revelation, visions, healing, interpretation of tongues, and so forth.

Experience has proven this true! Through God and the power of the Holy Ghost, every faithful Church member is given a spiritual gift that can be of benefit to mankind, but not everyone receives *every* gift.

It would be confusing if we all had the gift of prophecy for everyone else's life. It would be limiting if only a few had the gift of teaching and testifying of the gospel of Jesus Christ. Many are given the gift to heal or to be healed. Some must lean upon the strength of others, but they may have the gift to believe in others who bear witness that Jesus is the Christ, for example. In The Church of Jesus Christ of Latter-day Saints, spiritual gifts are available. This is one of the blessings for Church members and their loved ones—authority, know-how, and promises to accompany spiritual gifts that are so important to life. This means that as you need inspiration, healing, or renewal of faith, you can receive it through God's gifts.

References to Study

> Bible: Mark 16:17; Luke 10:17
> Book of Mormon: Alma 9:21
> Doctrine and Covenants 46:11–26

8. We believe the Bible to be the word of God as far as it is translated correctly; we also believe the Book of Mormon to be the word of God.

Bible scholars generally agree with the fact that the writings that make up today's Bible have not come down to us as they were in the beginning. Many errors occurred because of countless translations and translators—trained to a greater or lesser degree! Some sections were deliberately changed by designing and corrupt men.

In their original form, the books of the Bible reflected God's dealings and teachings among his children on earth at that time. Therefore, Latter-day Saints are taught to believe the Bible as far as it reflects truth witnessed by the power of the Holy Ghost or revelation by God to his modern prophets.

The Book of Mormon was translated by Joseph Smith from metal plates kept by appointed scribes among the generations of God's people in ancient America. The Testimony of the Three Witnesses in the preliminary pages of the Book of Mormon includes these words, "We . . . have seen the plates. . . . And we also know that they have been translated by the gift and power of God, for his voice hath declared it unto us; wherefore we know of a surety that the work is true." The prophet Moroni challenged all readers of the Book of Mormon to find out its truth for themselves: "And when ye shall receive these things, I would exhort you that ye would ask God, the Eternal Father, in the name of Christ, if these things are not true; and if ye shall ask with a sincere heart, with real intent, having faith in Christ, he will manifest the truth of it unto you, by the power of the Holy Ghost" (Moroni 10:4).

References to Study

> Bible: Isaiah 29:4; Ezekiel 37:15–20
> Book of Mormon: 1 Nephi 13:26
> Doctrine and Covenants 42:12

9. We believe all that God has revealed, all that He does now reveal, and we believe that He will yet reveal many great and important things pertaining to the Kingdom of God.

Joseph Smith's experience in the Sacred Grove proved that God the Father and Jesus Christ not only live but also that they care about people on earth and will continue to do so through their appointed and ordained prophets. God will also reveal truth to us individually. This means that continuing revelation is a special blessing given to Latter-day Saints. Because of this we not only know more about the workings of earthly things, we also are in a position to receive knowledge about spiritual things. There is still so much to learn!

We know that we are alive, but we know little about how death works.

We know that Christ lives, but we know nothing about how resurrection happens.

We marvel at the miracle of newborn babies, but we know nothing about when or how the spirit sent from heaven enters the body of an infant.

But, as members of the Lord's church, having received the gift of the Holy Ghost, we can knock, seek, ask, pray, and expect increase in spiritual understanding. This is the only way we can be truly effective in our efforts to help others.

References to Study

> Bible: Joel 2:28; John 5:39
> Book of Mormon: 1 Nephi 13:26; Mormon 8:26

10. We believe in the literal gathering of Israel and in the restoration of the Ten Tribes; that Zion (the New Jerusalem) will be built upon the American continent; that Christ will reign personally upon the earth; and, that the earth will be renewed and receive its paradisiacal glory.

This article of faith has four parts focusing on events prophesied long ago as being part of the last days.

(1) *The literal gathering.* In each dispensation of time, God has had a group of his children who were chosen to help in this cause. The gathering is important because then people are given the opportunity to know and do those things that will lead them back home to heaven and the presence of God.

Remember, the tribes of Israel were scattered across the earth and were lost to each other and lost to the beneficial aspects of God's saving principles. It may help to think of the "gathering" as a kind of colossal reunion of Heavenly Father's family!

The heads of the twelve tribes were Jacob's sons Reuben, Simeon, Levi, Judah, Issachar, and Zebulun (the sons of Leah); Dan and Naphtali (the sons of Bilhah); Gad and Asher (the sons of Zilpah); and Joseph and Benjamin (the sons of Jacob's beloved Rachel). Before Jacob—Father Israel—died, he gave each son a patriarchal or father's blessing that foretold the destinies of their posterity.

Members in good standing are worthy to be given a patriarchal blessing by one having authority to do so. Lineage—one's ancestral link to the twelve tribes of Israel—is declared at this time.

(2) *The New Jerusalem.* During the Millennium, there will be government under God with two world capitals. One will be Jerusalem in the Holy Land on Zion's hill, known as such since King David's reign. The other will be the New Jerusalem to be built in Jackson County, Missouri. It will be known as the City of Zion.

There are many scriptural references to these great centers of leadership. The law and the word of God will go forth from them. For example, in Isaiah 2:3 we read, "For out of Zion shall go forth the law, and the word of the Lord from Jerusalem."

(3) *Christ will reign.* When Christ comes again to earth to reign, peace will flood the earth and Satan will be bound. The scriptures are clear that no one knows the exact time of his coming but that it will be at the height of the world's wars and wickedness. This period of time is called the Millennium because it will last one thousand years.

(4) *Paradisiacal glory of the earth.* The earth will be renewed when Christ comes. It will be returned to its most glorious state—paradisiacal—and beauty and truth will sweep the earth as a flood.

People who join the Church are part of the gathering of Israel—part of the fulfillment of prophecy. To consider these promises about the future is to consider your part in all of this. You have been "gathered," and therefore you are chosen to help in this incredibly exciting and vital period of the history of the earth when Heavenly Father's children are at last gathered together to know and be known.

References to Study

    Bible: Deuteronomy 30:1–3; Matthew 24:31
    Book of Mormon: Ether 13:5–6
    Pearl of Great Price: Moses 7:62
    Turning Twelve or More: Living by the Articles of Faith (Elaine Cannon [Salt Lake City: Bookcraft, 1990], pp. 72–75)

11. We claim the privilege of worshiping Almighty God according to the dictates of our own conscience, and allow all men the same privilege, let them worship how, where, or what they may.

People can worship as they choose according to their agency. We honor this right. This is, of course, an important consideration for the developing attitude of the new member of the LDS church. You have joined these ranks of worship and left behind whatever doctrine or ceremony that is not compatible with the truth of The Church of Jesus Christ of Latter-day Saints. Remember, those who were with the Prophet Joseph Smith at the time of the formal organization of this church had worshipped in a variety of edifices and according to what was taught by the current preacher. On 6 April 1830 in Fayette, New York, a small gathering of people followed instructions from God to establish his church according to the principles and structure that would be right for his children in today's world. Since that day, membership of the Church of Jesus Christ has grown into the many millions. Its congregations are made up of people from the religions of the world, cast aside now in favor of the fulness and truth that the restored gospel of Jesus Christ provides.

People usually do the best they can with what they know and what they have. As we learn more of our fellowmen and what they hold sacred, we can better explain the gospel in their own frame of reference. The Latter-day Saint missionary or person sharing the truth will be able to explain the additional or more accurate gospel beliefs and behavior found only in the LDS church if they begin by pointing out the areas of belief that we have in common.

People worship in ways that differ a lot or a little from others. This eleventh article of faith reminds us that there are good people across the world who seek solace, forgiveness, and help from the only God they know after the manner they have been taught. Travel throughout the world reveals the similarity in each person's spiritual and temporal needs as well as the wide variety of modes of expression in the religious setting. This is why missionary work is so vital.

This Church helps others to know the true way to worship God and to understand that religion is an everyday, all year, lifetime pursuit to bring man to God!

Joseph Smith, the boy seeking to find out which church was true, recognized the confusion in his neighborhood—each church seeking membership from the townspeople. Joseph's answer came from God directly. He was told that he should join none of them, for they were all wrong. There followed the instruction, enlightenment, and spiritual training so that the full restoration could be made of God's tenets, commandments, ordinances, and understanding of the plan of life. This, of course, has been done, and revelation from God continues through his prophets in these latter days.

Meanwhile, it is wise to remember the eleventh article of faith so that we remain humble in our own knowledge of the fulness of God's gospel and the great blessing that comes and comes and comes for being members of The Church of Jesus Christ of Latter-day Saints. We strive to understand where others are coming from in order to better serve them and lead them.

This article of faith also expresses how much we value the divine gift of free agency.

References to Study

> Bible: Matthew 5:44–48; John 8:32–36
> Book of Mormon: Alma 21:22

12. We believe in being subject to kings, presidents, rulers, and magistrates, in obeying, honoring, and sustaining the law.

Surely this article of faith is self-explanatory. Wouldn't it be marvelous if all people held this idea as a sacred and wise guide for behavior and attitude? During war, this becomes an especially important philosophy as the draft for servicemen triggers conscientious objectors in many sectors and religions. LDS military people often find they can serve God—even do remarkable missionary work in teaching others the truth—while serving their country.

God's house is a house of order. In order to help ensure order, members need to become familiar with laws that govern the family, church, community, and nation. Wit, wisdom, and skills must be cultivated to not only sustain the current law and leaders but also improve the situation as needed. Many members of the Church in troubled countries outside the United States are gaining an increasing awareness of the importance of the twelfth article of faith.

References to Study

> Bible: Exodus 22:28; Proverbs 24:21
> Book of Mormon: Alma 1:14
> Doctrine and Covenants 134:5–9

13. We believe in being honest, true, chaste, benevolent, virtuous, and in doing good to all men; indeed, we may say that we follow the admonition of Paul—We believe all things, we hope all things, we have endured many things, and hope to be able to

endure all things. If there is anything virtuous, lovely, or of good report or praiseworthy, we seek after these things.

This is the "wrap-up" statement of belief. Latter-day Saints believe in continuing the pursuit of positive relationships and self-improvement, in delighting in the good things of life, and in enduring to the end. In order to make it in heaven, we must make it on earth and become people who will not disturb the peace of heaven and who will be comfortable there. Meanwhile, life is more rewarding and successful when lived according to the thirteenth article of faith.

Virtuously living is the only way to avoid regret.

You are what you eat, read, think, do, and associate with. The basis for the good life is to seek only after those things that come well recommended and that foster the purity you need for the Spirit of God to dwell within you.

References to Study

Bible: Matthew 7:12; 1 Corinthians 13:4–7; Philippians 4:8; James 1:27

Doctrine and Covenants 132:52

What Does All This Mean to You?

The Articles of Faith will help you be happier and wiser as you live as an "example of the believers, in word, in conversation, in charity, in spirit, in faith, in purity" (1 Timothy 4:12). The same holds true today just as it did then for the disciples of Christ in his day.

As a member of God's restored church, you have the advantage of:

- Precious perspective of life and life eternal, so your goals are higher.
- Accessing programs to ensure spiritual, mental, and social growth, according to God's will for you.
- Receiving ordinances and opportunities that enrich the soul and prepare you for eternal life.
- Understanding the plan of life, which promotes increased endurance in times of trouble or temptation.
- Being awakened to the responsibility and satisfaction that is yours in being charitable and helpful to others, particularly those less fortunate than you.

- Becoming more effective in explaining and testifying of the saving truths of the gospel and the reality of God.
- Talking with God through prayer more frequently, effectively, and fervently.

President Ezra Taft Benson said that as a boy he learned a poem that remained with him throughout his life. It may be inspirational for you, as well.

> I know not by what methods rare
> But this I know, God answers prayer.
> I know that He has given His word,
> Which tells me prayer is always heard,
> And will be answered, soon or late.
> And so I pray and calmly wait.
> I know not if the blessing sought
> Will come in just the way I thought;
> But leave my prayers with Him alone,
> Whose will is wiser than my own,
> Assured that He will grant my quest,
> Or send some answer far more blessed.

(Eliza M. Hickok, "Prayer," quoted in Ezra Taft Benson, "Pray Always," *Ensign*, February 1990, p. 5.)

16

The Standard Works

For almost every need, emotion, challenge, and understanding, there is a scripture in the Church of Jesus Christ that comes bursting through like a personal answer to prayer. Some scriptures are warmly comforting. Some are commanding. Some are especially literary in language and phrasing—beautiful to read regardless of message. Some are so pertinent to the structure of life itself that they are thrilling to discover!

The standard works of the Church are those books containing the word of God that have been declared by God as being basic to religious belief. The King James Version of the Old and New Testaments is authorized for reference in the LDS church. We believe this edition to be true as far as it is translated correctly.

The Book of Mormon is beloved in a special way by Latter-day Saints. It is a volume of holy scripture comparable to the Bible. It is composed of records kept by God's appointed servants from generation to generation of their relationship with God and his teachings to them personally or by revelation. These ancient records were made on metal plates that were later abridged by the Nephite prophet Mormon and his son Moroni. On 18 September 1823, Joseph Smith was guided to these records by Moroni, then an angel or resurrected being. Under admonition from God and through the power of the Holy

Ghost, Joseph translated them. It was a miracle for the great good of mankind and is a second witness or testimony of Christ in addition to the Bible.

Members of the Church are encouraged by the prophet and other leaders and teachers to read the Book of Mormon daily not only as a means of fully understanding God's word but also because this study brings a person closer to Christ. Through continued study the time comes when reading the Book of Mormon becomes a time of closeness with the Savior, as if he were speaking directly to your heart.

The Book of Mormon is used as a proselyting tool with nonmembers, who are invited to read the book, to ponder its message in their hearts, and to pray unto God for confirmation of its validity. Through the power of the Holy Ghost, this spiritual witness will occur for those who ask in honest faith. You may have been through this experience yourself, but it would be good to periodically read again Moroni 10:3–5.

The Doctrine and Covenants contains revelations from God given to Joseph Smith and to others called of God to succeed him as President of The Church of Jesus Christ of Latter-day Saints. It is full of precious doctrine for our day in the fulness of times and restoration of the true gospel.

The Pearl of Great Price includes selections from the writings of Moses and father Abraham. Much of the detailed understanding regarding the Creation and the plan of life, for example, is available through this book. Other religions do not have this knowledge in their own religious literature!

Also included in these scriptures are the story of the First Vision and the Articles of Faith, both written by Joseph Smith, as well as his translation or revision of a portion of the Gospel of Matthew.

In the standard works is a wealth of wisdom, relevant guidance, inspiration, and everlasting principles. The word of God is thus given for the good of mankind in working out our own salvation and preparing for ultimate exaltation.

Because these scriptures form the basis of our way of life as members of the LDS church, we refer to them constantly. You, like others in the Church, undoubtedly will collect your own motivating scriptures.

Learn to use the scriptures by knowing how to read references. The name of the book comes first. Then the chapter or section number follows. A colon separates the verse number from the chapter or section.

For example:

- Doctrine and Covenants 21:6
- 3 Nephi 11:5 (Book of Mormon)
- James 1:5 (New Testament)

The standard works of the Church have cross-reference information that leads the reader from a certain word in a verse to the footnotes at the bottom of the page. These show additional scripture references in other volumes that are relative.

Study the scriptures consistently each day. Read from front to back or use the index or Topical Guide to research the subject that you happen to need or have a special interest in at the moment. Underline and memorize significant verses. Some people like to highlight those words that directly refer to or are spoken by the Lord.

When Anthony Joseph Wirthlin Cannon was eight years old, he was baptized and confirmed in the historic font in the Tabernacle on Temple Square in Salt Lake City, Utah. There was a little program before the baptism. As Anthony's grandfather, Elder Joseph B. Wirthlin of the Quorum of the Twelve Apostles, was speaking, he used one of the Articles of Faith. Anthony had memorized them all in preparation for this exciting event in his life. As his grandfather spoke, Anthony moved his lips and silently recited the fourth article of faith perfectly. Then as Elder Wirthlin referred to a scripture in the Bible, Anthony quickly picked up his own personal scriptures that he had received that day as a birthday present. His father helped him find the scripture in the Bible, and Anthony followed along.

Little children can learn the scriptures early in life, and it is a fine tradition in some families to make the eighth birthday a time for presenting their child with his own copy of the standard works. Adults should have their personal set of the standard works that they read daily and take to Church meetings.

When you read the scriptures, you draw near to the Savior and feel his goodness and love. While searching for his will, his word, or a perspective on a certain gospel topic, you are in a listening or receiving mood. You will feel his Spirit and his approbation of your efforts. Reading the scriptures prepares you for praying, and praying before you read the scriptures increases your focus and understanding.

Nephi wrote, "Wherefore, ye must press forward with a steadfast-
ness in Christ, having a perfect brightness of hope, and a love of God
and of all men. Wherefore, if ye shall press forward, feasting upon the
word of Christ, and endure to the end, behold, thus saith the Father:
Ye shall have eternal life." (2 Nephi 32:20.)

17

Questions and Answers

Now, after all that has been said and done, what comes next?

Thanks to the Lord Jesus Christ, your cup "runneth o'er." Armed now with a new heart awakened to the plans and blessings the Creator has in store for you, forward you go. Hope is your banner, and the people in the Church are your cheerleaders and teammates. They want you to make it, as God does! Ahead is the broad path of learning, giving, feeling, being—the path of becoming a disciple of Christ.

The sustaining power of God has watched over you through a mighty change in your life—through baptism, confirmation, and perhaps a host of challenging, stimulating experiences in a new church. Now, practically speaking, your free agency needs to be bolstered with information. You probably have a lot of questions that require answers that might modify your behavior in certain settings and at times succor your self-esteem.

Q. What is expected of me now?

A. The prophet Alma gave us a brief but important scriptural explanation of what is expected of each of us: "For behold, this life is the time for men to prepare to meet God; yea, behold the day of this life is the day for men to perform their labors. . . . Do not procrastinate the day . . . which is given us to prepare for eternity." (Alma 34:32–33.)

Your basic goal should be to prepare to meet God! The Church's mission is to invite all to come unto Christ and be perfected in him so that they will ultimately qualify for that great day of reunion with Deity. Keep active in the Church programs and continue your prayerful study of the scriptures so that your understanding will grow of what it is you are to do, learn, and apply to your life. When you are in full devotion, Satan cannot destroy you. But remember, he would like to!

The Doctrine and Covenants contains counsel specifically for us and our day:

> And I now give unto you a commandment to beware concerning yourselves, to give diligent heed to the words of eternal life.
>
> For you shall live by every word that proceedeth forth from the mouth of God.
>
> For the word of the Lord is truth, and whatsoever is truth is light, and whatsoever is light is Spirit, even the Spirit of Jesus Christ.
>
> And the Spirit giveth light to every man [and woman] that cometh into the world; and the Spirit enlighteneth every man through the world, that hearkeneth to the voice of the Spirit.
>
> And every one that hearkeneth to the voice of the Spirit cometh unto God, even the Father. (Doctrine and Covenants 84:43–47.)

What is expected of you? Only those things that will be for your good, your joy! Be a lively member. Build the power of godliness in you. Draw upon the powers of heaven. When you learn truth, share it with others. Be spiritually and morally clean, and keep close to the Lord—do this no matter what else is going on in your life. Be loyal to the Church and to its leaders, who are doing their best as servants of the Lord to help each of us develop and progress happily in life.

The member's manual is to some extent the Doctrine and Covenants. In section 20 we learn the duty of members after they are received by baptism. To summarize the revelation, members manifest before the Church that they are worthy of the privilege of membership in God's church by a godly walk and conversation, by walking in holiness before the Lord, by bringing their children before the elders of the church to receive a name and a blessing by the laying on of hands, and by seeing that children are baptized and confirmed at the age of accountability when they are capable of repentance.

Q. We've been taught that "strait is the way and narrow is the gate" to heaven. Does this mean my life as a Latter-day Saint will be confining?

A. The gospel promises the abundant life. You are free to choose from life's richly varied menu. Sharpen your focus so that selective choices will be pleasing to God. An attitude of "Thy will, not mine" is good to cultivate.

There is a yardstick by which to measure your choices. Use it! "For behold, the Spirit of Christ is given to every [person], that he may know good from evil; . . . for every thing which inviteth to do good, and to persuade to believe in Christ, is sent forth by the power and gift of Christ; . . . but whatsoever thing persuadeth men to do evil, and believe not in Christ, and deny him, and serve not God, then ye may know with a perfect knowledge it is of the devil." (Moroni 7:16–17.)

When a choice is closer to the side of worldliness or is tied to self-weakening, all your antennae should be up to their full height. Use such warnings to secure your access through the narrow gate of purity and wisdom. You see, when you become entangled in sin, you have no more freedom of choice. In the words of God: "Abide ye in the liberty wherewith ye are made free; entangle not yourselves in sin, but let your hands be clean, until the Lord comes" (Doctrine and Covenants 88:86).

Q. What happens on Sunday?

A. The Sabbath is the Lord's day. Since Sunday is a day holy unto the Lord, remember to keep it holy. You might consider dressing and acting as if Jesus were walking along beside you.

Volumes have been written to prescribe Sunday activities, but a good standard is simply that the Lord's day should be lived the Lord's way, which isn't really limiting when you think about all the good the Savior did. Oh, the good you can do with such a day! Oh, the things you can learn to secure your access through the narrow gate of purity, wisdom, and happiness!

Church attendance is critical for Latter-day Saints. If anything, followers of Christ know there is much to learn, and they understand that this knowledge is vital to growth and joy.

Q. What is it really like at Church meetings? Will I fit in?

A. As you become involved in Church activity, make it a point to introduce yourself and to find out about others. You may discover other newcomers. Open yourself to the love of these people who believe as you want to believe. Congregations can change often with new people joining, so after a time or two you will be on the welcoming end. Cast your bread upon this water, and it will come back to you in a welcome flood.

Walk in on a Latter-day Saint meeting where congregational singing is under way, and suddenly your soul is lightened. There is a spirit there. Mormon hymns are inspirational, strengthening, uplifting, and educational. For example, when you join in the singing of "O My Father" and come to the verse about having a Father and Mother in Heaven, you might be reminded of a truth most comforting and mind stretching.

You will be aware of many children in the meetings. Latter-day Saints believe in bearing and rearing children. They also believe a child should be trained and taught from the first. On Sunday, children and youth are part of the meetings—part of hymn singing, prayer, public speaking, and gospel study with state-of-the-art manuals prepared at Church headquarters. And yes, children are taught to get used to a great many meetings, most of which are informal.

There is a spirit of well-being when Latter-day Saints gather. Friendliness and happiness radiate as the people mingle before the meetings begin and proper reverence is observed. In such a setting, members feel welcome. Support and help are available to you through this inspired Church structure.

Q. Will I have to do anything at the meetings?

A. Probably! Maybe you won't have to do much at first, but this is a lay church, so there is extensive congregation participation. Members are given opportunities to participate in various ways in Sunday meetings, whether it is the sacrament meeting, a report or planning meeting, choir practice, or classroom instruction. Latter-day Saints believe that contention is of the devil (see Helaman 16:22). Gracious relationships are nurtured. The rooms of the meeting place bustle with classes for all age groups. Volunteers are called to be helpers. They teach, conduct, pray, lead the singing, speak, expound, and participate in special ordinances. The Spirit is invited to be present, and gratitude for such a gift is expressed through prayer at the opening and closing of each new meeting or class. Through these activities, you'll find that your testimony and commitment to the gospel are strengthened. And as you participate, your love for the Lord and for those you serve will grow.

Q. What motivates all this activity?

A. Latter-day Saints take great value in phrases such as "endure to the end," "the glory of God is intelligence," and "learn how to live celestial laws in a telestial world." These reflect the members' faith in a full life hereafter. They believe the quality and activity of our eternal life will be largely determined by performance on earth.

Here is a good life-direction scripture to think about: "Wash you, make you clean; put away the evil of your doings from before mine eyes; cease to do evil; learn to do well; seek judgment, relieve the oppressed, judge the fatherless, plead for the widow; . . . reason together, . . . if ye be willing and obedient, ye shall eat the good of the land." (Isaiah 1:16–19).

Q. What about spiritual growth?

A. Uplifting spiritual meetings or intimate gatherings of family and friends provide great strength, growth, and comfort. However, your individual spirituality, personal knowledge, and ever-growing testimony will increase in your own soul because of your own efforts and God's grace. Your efforts will be enhanced by your pleas for help from the Lord.

It is interesting to learn that two people can sit side by side in the same fast and testimony meeting, and one will come out marveling about the spiritual quality of the meeting, while the other will not receive the same signals at all. We are each responsible for inviting the Spirit into our lives.

Q. Is Latter-day Saint social life all family oriented?

A. The Church's program is structured to implement God's plan of salvation for his children. Thus, the Church covers every vital aspect of life. Built into the system is consuming, interesting involvement for every one of Heavenly Father's children. Some events are required, some are optional. And the list of possibilities includes such things as family history, leadership training, chorister skills development, instructional visitors' centers, service, welfare duties, temple work, conferences, motivational retreats, missionary work, sports, camping, field trips to Church historical sites, and continuing educational opportunities such as special study courses in Israel or campus education weeks for nonregistered students.

Yes, you'll soon be living the life of the "anxiously engaged" because the Church of Jesus Christ keeps you incredibly, blessedly busy in worthwhile pursuits.

Q. What if I make a mistake?

A. Even with the best of intentions, you can't expect that perfection will fall like a cloak on your shoulders overnight. Perfection is a process that continues into eternity. If you make a mistake, the nature of it probably determines your action. Draw close to the Lord, and talk it over with him. You'll be guided to get help from your bishop if necessary.

Repent. Keep believing. Keep trying. Keep the faith! "Endure to the end," you know, is a good creed. But look for joy by counting your blessings. Keep a humble spirit. Be patient with the imperfections of others as you pray that they will be patient with your own growth.

Q. How do members deal with tithes and offerings, the Word of Wisdom, and other such commandments?

A. Members are constantly trying.

As a new member you may need to set some new goals and establish a system for budgeting contributions and maintaining high personal standards when you are away from the Church setting.

There are no collection plates in The Church of Jesus Christ of Latter-day Saints. The Church is financed through the individual tithes and offerings of members. Tithing is ten percent of your increase and is usually paid monthly to the bishop of your ward. It is a very private matter between you, the Lord, and your bishop. When you ask for a bishop's recommend for the temple, one of the questions he will ask is whether you are a full-tithe payer.

We believe that all that we have is from the hand of God. Therefore, it is a privilege to return a tenth of our increase to help build the kingdom of God on earth. Inevitable blessings come from such devotion and obedience. Personal conversion to this principle and its accompanying blessings comes from putting the principle to the test. Obey the commandment and see for yourself. Encourage your children in this principle as soon as possible, such as paying tithing on an allowance or when they earn a little money raking leaves or baby tending.

Keeping the Word of Wisdom as outlined in the eighty-ninth section of the Doctrine and Covenants is also a requirement for obtaining a recommend but not for all Church service. This too is a matter between you, the Lord, and your Church leader.

The Word of Wisdom is a law given for our own good. The world is just barely catching up with Latter-day Saints on the evils of smoking and drinking, for example. Joseph Smith received that revelation 150 years ago. Strength to live the Word of Wisdom comes in response to fervent prayer. Many are the success stories of this principle. Understanding why these health laws are required and how they affect spiritual growth and health will help strengthen your commitment to obey them. You see, for example, that when you are blessed with the gift of the Holy Ghost and the wonderful blessing it is, you are anxious to abide the counsel that it will not dwell in an unclean tabernacle.

Q. What about revelations and free agency?

A. The President of the Church is also the prophet of God on earth through whom direct revelation comes for the Church, world-wide. Members are asked to raise an arm to the square and vote to sustain the prophet and other General Authorities. So if you can't agree with something you hear them officially teach, perhaps you haven't grown spiritually enough to trust in the servant of the Lord. Maybe you need to get personal revelation yourself by studying the problem, searching the scriptures, and earnestly praying to the Lord. Sometimes you must abide for a time before you understand the counsel. Sometimes you just abide! You do this because the system is God inspired but man implemented. People who serve and people who follow have their agency and are well-meaning, conscientious, and imperfect persons trying to grow in godliness. Wait upon the Lord to put your mind at ease.

One of the most moving moments at any conference in the Church is witnessing the common consent procedure. As the signifying vote is called for by a show of hands, rarely is there a dissenting vote, though always the opportunity is given because free agency is honored.

Q. What about new covenants and old habits?

A. One of the miracles of covenants and the accompanying under-standing of how they relate to life is that spiritual strength inevitably comes! Strength to change undesirable old habits follows. Most mem-bers learn things a step at a time, line upon line, grace for grace from God. Thanks be to God for repentance! Consider this scripture as rele-vant: "I give unto you these sayings that you may understand and know how to worship, and know what you worship, that you may come unto the Father in my name, and in due time receive of his ful-ness. For if you keep my commandments you shall receive of his ful-ness, and be glorified in me as I am in the Father; therefore I say unto you, you shall receive grace for grace." (Doctrine and Covenants 93: 19–20.)

With baptism came the new life, new change, new aura. The Lord will help you, and so will the good people of the Church who also are trying to be valiant. Taking the sacrament each Sunday reminds you of the sacred covenants you made with God. Attending church and studying the scriptures daily keeps you in touch with your new goals. Daily prayer morning and night keeps you in touch with Heavenly Father. The one person who can always be with you as you strive to keep your covenants is the Holy Ghost.

Q. What if I fail at this new life?

A. Fail? You have just been given a clean slate, a new life through baptism. You are supported by the structure, principles, and people of The Church of Jesus Christ of Latter-day Saints. God himself is waiting to be gracious and help if you'll but use your agency to turn to him. You will not fail ultimately with all of that going for you. Oh, you might have a setback or two, but if you hold on to the iron rod, or the word of God, difficult times will pass.

President David O. McKay wrote some great wisdom for times of self-examination when failure stares you in the face. He said: "Nobody wants to fall as a failure along life's highway, but many do. Some fail because of outward circumstances that defeat and thwart their plans. Some fail because of inward circumstances—insincerity, pride, greed, lust, jealousy, etc. Some fail for lack of first-rate ambitions; they are unwilling to face an honest self-appraisal and accept themselves as they are. Some fail because they adopt the wrong means to realize the right goal—poor headwork that does not match a good heart in their necessary cooperation."

Q. Sometimes I feel stupid in Sunday School class. I get confused if there is a discussion in which not everyone agrees, including me. What should I do?

A. Differences of opinion are bound to exist, even among members of the Church. Such differences are a natural result of free agency, varied personal background, orientations, and level of spiritual development, for example. We are, however, all striving for unity in basic belief and doctrine. Opinions are one thing; scripture and the voice of the prophet quite another. Remember that we are united in love and concern for each other. Humility includes tender encouragement to keep on working toward perfection. If someone thinks differently from you, perhaps you should talk with the teacher after class.

Always take your scriptures to class with you, and review the scheduled lesson subject ahead of time, if you can.

Q. There are so many wonderful people in the Church. Will I ever be equal to them? It all seems so hard.

A. You are right, it is different in this church. Vive la différence!

As to Latter-day Saint life seeming *hard,* the Lord has told us that his yoke is easy. To live by the principles your Creator established for your life is easier, in the long walk, than living another way. Obeying—following the happier course set by the One who knows best what is best—is a happier route than sorrow and shame and repentance.

One difficulty among all human beings is that the spirit may be willing but the flesh is often weak. But the scripture "I can do all things through Christ which strengtheneth me" (Philippians 4:13) is a belief to bolster a conquering, enduring attitude.

Take it a step at a time, a day at a time, a prayer at a time. God will help those who want to be helped to achieve the quality of immortality that he has in mind for you. Through Christ's atonement, all mankind is saved, all will be resurrected. The quality of eternal life is another matter, and Latter-day Saints know this more significantly than others.

Already you know a lot about eternal life and the gospel that prepares us for it. But knowledge does not guarantee performance, whether it has to do with weight loss, quitting smoking, or religious life. Studies and personal experience show that internalizing the gospel principles as you learn them and then applying them to life can bring about desired changes.

Q. What about Satan?

A. Well, what about Satan? He is a reality. As real as Jesus, but not nearly as powerful.

Latter-day Saints believe in the reality of Satan and in the War in Heaven before this world was. This was a lining up of the forces of good and evil. In mortality we must now subdue and eliminate at last the shackles and miserable fetters of Satan's temptations. His mission is to thwart the kingdom of God and its work on earth. Satan's designs are to get us to sin, knowing that when we sin we separate ourselves from God. Then we are without the Spirit and the guidance and the interest in the Church programs and gospel principles that we need to move along.

It isn't just the knowledge of God and Satan that makes a difference in prayers or in behavior. It is also knowledge of self. In the

Doctrine and Covenants we read that keeping God's commandments brings truth and light until that person is glorified and knoweth all things: "Man was also in the beginning with God. Intelligence, or the light of truth, was not created or made, neither indeed can be." (Doctrine and Covenants 93:29.) Satan was in the beginning, too, and knew enough to have become a god if his attitude had been better! Don't make the same mistake yourself.

Q. Will I ever be rid of Satan's works in my life?

A. Satan will not be bound until the Millennium. Meanwhile it remains for each of us to fortify ourselves against his efforts by putting on the whole armor of God. Beware of Satan, and be aware that he isn't too interested in those already in his stronghold of despair, disgrace, and lost opportunities. His mightiest war is raging against the citizens of the kingdom of God on earth. Now that you have joined those ranks, he will keep hovering about in your life. Holding Satan at bay is best accomplished through a life strictly lived according to gospel principles.

Q. How will I know I am "making it"?

A. Keep close to your sources of strength if you sense a weakening of your will or behavior. These sources include your priesthood leaders, your member contacts with the same ideals, and certainly the Lord. Dare to pour out your need from a contrite heart!

After your faith is tried come the blessings, the miracles, the witness.

Remember the parable of the prodigal son who at last returned home? The father, seeing him afar off, rushed to welcome the son home. So will it be for each of us and our Heavenly Father. We will know we are "making it" as we keep turning back to him; he will rush forth to welcome us, to bless us, to celebrate our progress! And he will greet us warmly as many times as it takes.

Epilogue

Being a member of The Church of Jesus Christ of Latter-day Saints is an experience that constantly reawakens one's mind and heart to the sweet and saving ways of Jesus—in our behalf.

In today's church, just as it was in the Savior's early church, members are encouraged to try to be more like him. Then what a glorious world we would live in—peace and joy among the disciples of Christ! We would exemplify daily Paul's charge to Timothy: "Be thou an example of the believers, in word, in conversation, in charity, in spirit, in faith, in purity. . . . Neglect not the gift that is in thee, which was given thee by prophecy, with the laying on of the hands." (1 Timothy 4:12, 14.)

The highest of all ideals are found in the gospel of Jesus Christ. The person who follows after him most closely is inclined to greatness and a peaceful spirit.

Heavenly Father's plan of happiness provides wonderful direction and support for your efforts to follow after Jesus Christ. It ensures you an abundance in life if you but participate in it fully. If you don't, the measure of despair that you can suffer will be considerable!

Now, consider this most remarkable promise, which is actually the basis of this book. If you do what the Lord has commanded and obey his guiding Spirit, then "the gates of hell shall not prevail against you"! "The Lord God will disperse the powers of darkness from before you"! He will "cause the heavens to shake for your good"! (See Doctrine and Covenants 21:4–6.)

May you through your choices now gather the blessings of inspired living within the fold of the Church. Surely you will make fewer mistakes and feel less temptation. You will know more joy.

I give thanks for each one of you who joins in the glorious mission of assisting in the building of a noble people—stalwart individuals, caring citizens, responsible husbands and wives, benevolent and affectionate family members—who adhere to the wise, right, rewarding ways of our example, Jesus Christ.

Because of your enthusiastic participation in the gospel and the choice experiences of the Church of Jesus Christ, you will grow ever more like the Savior.

You not only will be a survivor in life, you will prevail.

You will be able to cope effectively with whatever comes to you.

You will qualify for exaltation—ultimately.

You will be guided through the land mines of this life until you are safely dead, as we say, and are welcomed into the loving arms of God. Millions of members can so testify.

This is true! This all is true!

Glossary

Aaronic Priesthood: known as the lesser priesthood because it is a preparation for the greater priesthood, or the Melchizedek Priesthood. Those who faithfully hold the Aaronic Priesthood are in a position to have angels minister to them and are of special assistance to the ward bishop, and as priests are authorized to baptize by immersion. A worthy young man is eligible for this priesthood at the age of twelve.

Anoint: to apply oil to the head of someone in preparation for blessing them. Today, anointings are most commonly performed on the sick.

Apostasy: departure from the true gospel of Jesus Christ; may involve individuals or large groups. The Christian apostasy began not long after Christ's crucifixion and continued to develop following the deaths of his Apostles. The world remained without the gospel until it was restored through Joseph Smith.

Apostle: one called to be a special witness of Christ to all the world. Today twelve men constitute the Quorum of the Twelve Apostles, and they participate in administering the affairs of the Church. Each is a prophet and knows by personal revelation that Jesus Christ is the Son of the living God.

Articles of Faith: thirteen statements outlining the basic beliefs of The Church of Jesus Christ of Latter-day Saints. Joseph Smith prepared them in response to a request by an Illinois newsman. They were first printed in the Church newspaper, the *Times and Seasons,* in 1842.

Atonement: the great sacrifice Jesus Christ made when he took all the sins of all mankind upon himself and by his death and resurrection brought all of us the resurrection. The Atonement is the foundation upon which all gospel principles rest; it was necessary because of the fall of Adam and Eve. To atone is to redeem, to pay the price or penalty for; it is the way of bringing mankind back into the presence of God.

Authority: in the Church, the right to preside, to carry out certain assigned duties, or to perform specific ordinances. Priesthood authority, which is given to all worthy males, is granted not because of status, position, or education but in line with Paul's expression: "No man taketh this honour unto himself, but he that is called of God, as was Aaron" (Hebrews 5:4).

Baptism for the dead: baptism of a living person who acts as proxy, or in behalf of, one who died without this saving ordinance.

Bishop: the head of members in a geographical area known as a ward. He holds the Melchizedek Priesthood and is ordained to be a common judge in Zion (see Doctrine and Covenants 107:74).

Book of Mormon: sacred scripture recorded prior to A.D. 421; an abridged account of God's children in ancient America, translated from metal plates by Joseph Smith as part of the restoration of the gospel; another witness for Jesus Christ; contains the doctrines of salvation.

Born in the covenant: offspring of parents who have been sealed together in the covenant of marriage in the temple. These children are automatically sealed to their parents; if they and their parents live worthily they may remain together throughout eternity.

Called: in the religious sense, to be chosen by God or those inspired and authorized by him to serve in a particular office or assignment.

Comforter: another name for the Holy Ghost. On the day before he was crucified, Jesus promised to send his disciples a Comforter to be with them while he was away from them (see John 14:16, 26).

Confirmation: an ordinance following baptism that bestows the gift of the Holy Ghost upon a person and grants him or her membership in the Church. Often the authorized administrators performing this ordinance may be led by the Spirit to pronounce certain blessings and exhortations.

Covenant: a sacred promise; an agreement between two or more persons that each will do certain things.

Disciple: one who follows; especially a follower of Jesus. Disciples are companions in the work of the kingdom of heaven on earth.

Dispensation: a period of time during which God reveals the doctrines of the gospel through his prophets. The dispensation of the fulness of times began when the gospel was restored through Joseph Smith. It is the final dispensation, an age in which the Lord will "gather together in one all things in Christ, both which are in heaven, and which are on earth." (See Ephesians 1:10; Doctrine and Covenants 27:13.)

Eternal life: the highest level of life beyond the grave; exaltation obtained through the grace of Christ and a person's righteous attitude and behavior on earth; life in the celestial kingdom, forever in the presence of God.

Evangelist: in the Church sense, an ordained patriarch.

Faith: total belief; in this case, conviction and trust in God the Father and in his Son Jesus Christ. "Faith is not to have a perfect knowledge of things; therefore if ye have faith ye hope for things which are not seen, which are true" (Alma 32:21).

Family home evening: a time set aside by the family for prayer, gospel study, singing, and other activities so that unity and mutual love may be enjoyed. The Church curriculum department has prepared a manual to be used for family home evening.

Fast: to abstain from eating or drinking for a period of time while drawing close to the Lord. A true and humble fast is accompanied by "rejoicing and prayer," as it says in Doctrine and Covenants 59:14.

Fast offerings: contributions given to the bishop of the ward on fast Sunday, usually the first Sunday of each month. The contributions most commonly equal the value of the meals skipped during the fast and are used for the needy.

Free agency: The God-given right each person has to make his or her own choices between good and evil. The Prophet Joseph Smith taught that people should be taught correct principles that they might govern themselves.

General conference: a meeting for the worldwide membership of the Church, held semiannually in April and October; broadcast live from the Salt Lake Tabernacle on Temple Square by satellite to many nations and translated in many languages; a gathering under the direction of the First Presidency for the purpose of edifying, educating, and uplifting the Saints, worshipping the Lord, and reporting on the status of the Church.

Godhead: the supreme governing power on earth and in heaven; the three exalted Beings—Heavenly Father, his Son Jesus Christ, and the Holy Ghost, who are individual personages but one in purpose.

Home teachers: generally, two priesthood holders assigned to represent the bishop in the home of a family or individual, bringing a greeting and a message; available to help meet spiritual or temporal needs. Appropriately done, home teaching can help bring about righteousness among the people. (See Doctrine and Covenants 20: 42–54.)

Immortality: unending, everlasting life; living forever beyond this life.

Israel: literally, "God rules" or "God shines." Jacob, son of Isaac, was called Israel, and his posterity became known as the house of Israel. Members of the Church today are of the lineage of Israel, whether by birth or by baptism. They have the responsibility for "the gathering of Israel" by bringing the gospel message to all people. Righteous members of the house of Israel are eligible for the blessings God promised their forefathers.

Laying on of hands: the placing of the hands of the Lord's authorized servants on a person's head in order to bestow blessings, ordinations, callings, anointings, and so on, according to the order of God.

Lineage: ancestry by blood or adoption in the house of Israel. See "Israel." All Latter-day Saints are members of the house of Israel, and through patriarchal blessings they learn which tribes of Israel they belong to. "As inheritors of the blessings of Jacob, it is the privilege of the gathered remnant of Jacob to receive their own patriarchal blessings and, by faith, to be blessed equally with the ancients" (Bruce R. McConkie, *Mormon Doctrine,* [Salt Lake City: Bookcraft, 1966], p. 558).

Melchizedek Priesthood: the higher, or greater, priesthood; the power and keys to all spiritual blessings of the Church. Named for the great high priest in ancient times to avoid too frequent repetition of the name of Deity, this priesthood's full name is the Holy Priesthood after the Order of the Son of God.

Mormon: a Nephite prophet and military commander (circa A.D. 310–385) who abridged the ancient records which were translated and gathered into the Book of Mormon. Today *Mormon* is a nickname for a member of The Church of Jesus Christ of Latter-day Saints.

Ordained: given authority in the priesthood by the laying on of hands by God's appointed servants.

Ordinance: something decreed by Deity and formalized in a ceremony, such as baptism, marriage, or the temple endowment.

Patriarchal blessing: a blessing given by an ordained patriarch and recorded in Church archives; what God has to say to us individually regarding our mission on earth, our lineage, and the promises and blessings in store for us according to our faithfulness.

Pearl of Great Price: a volume of scripture containing some of Joseph Smith's translations and writings.

Plan of salvation: the plan of life given to us by Heavenly Father and implemented by Jesus Christ; a plan that trains us, gives us opportunities to gain knowledge and to increase in spirituality, and has as its goal preparation for exaltation or eternal life.

Prophet: the Twelve Apostles and the members of the First Presidency of The Church of Jesus Christ of Latter-day Saints are prophets, seers, and revelators, but the President of the Church is considered "the prophet" and the ultimate authority on earth to receive God's direction for the Church.

Restoration: the act of making whole again; bringing something back as it was. The restoration of the gospel of Jesus Christ began with the first vision of Joseph Smith and continued with the inspired organization of the Church in 1830. It restored the ordinances and teachings of the ancient Church necessary for the immortality and eternal life of mankind.

Resurrection: the reuniting of the physical body with the spirit body after death.

Sacrament: an ordinance of the gospel of Jesus Christ to renew covenants made with him; members take the sacrament of bread and water in remembrance of the flesh and blood of Jesus Christ, who sacrificed his life for us. (See Moroni 4:3 and 5:2 for the sacramental prayers that Christ gave to the Nephite people and that we use today.)

Satan: Lucifer, the devil, the adversary. Satan was a spirit child of Heavenly Father as Jesus was and as we were. Because he was disobedient to Heavenly Father he was cast out of heaven, thus losing his chance to have a body on earth. In misguided anger, he and his followers try to tempt people who have bodies and to lure them away from Christ and eternal life.

Savior: Jesus Christ, the Son of God; firstborn of Heavenly Father's spirit children and his Only Begotten in the flesh, miraculously born to Mary; the only perfect being ever to live on earth. He is called the Savior because, through his suffering and death, he saves us from our sins if we repent. He enables us to return to the presence of God.

Scriptures: the word of God that he has revealed to his prophets. The Church speaks of the scriptures as the standard works—the Bible, the Book of Mormon, the Doctrine and Covenants, and the Pearl of Great Price—as well as revelations given to the prophets in our day. (See the eighth and ninth articles of faith.)

Sealing: binding, bonding, making permanent through the power of the priesthood. Acts that are sealed on earth are recognized in heaven.

Second Coming: that time when Christ will come to earth again to live and will personally reign in glory, when he will be known to all men.

Soul: the spirit together with the human body. After the resurrection, the spirit and body will become forever inseparable.

Spiritual gifts: personal abilities and powers which are gifts from God following the faith and obedience of his children. In 1 Corinthians 12:31, the faithful are reminded to seek spiritual gifts.

Temple: the house of God; a holy edifice dedicated for the performance of sacred ordinances, rites, and ceremonies which pertain to the salvation and exaltation of men and women in the kingdom of heaven. Entry is only to those who qualify for a recommend of worthiness from their bishop.

Testimony: personal belief, accompanied by the witness of the Holy Ghost, in the reality and divinity of Jesus Christ and the truthfulness of the restored gospel and of the Church.

Tithing: one-tenth of the increase of each member of the Church, which is contributed voluntarily and is used to fund the activities of the Church. *Increase* refers to one's salary or inheritances, wages, increase in herds, flocks, crops, and so on.

Tongues: speaking in tongues or translating them for the spiritual growth of those in the kingdom of God on earth. Speaking in tongues might involve speaking in the pure language of God as a manifestation of his Spirit, or the ability to speak or understand a foreign language for a period of time in order to help do the work of the Lord.

Transgression: violation of a law.

Urim and Thummim: an instrument prepared by God to assist man in gaining revelation from the Lord and to help in translating records written in unknown languages.

Visiting teachers: women from the Relief Society who go in pairs to visit the women of the Church in their homes to see to their spiritual and temporal welfare.

Zion: God's people always have been known as Zion; also, a place where his people dwell. In latter-day revelation, Zion is defined as "the pure in heart" (see Doctrine and Covenants 97:21).